THE BIG DATA REVOLUTION

The world is changing, are you ready?

Jason Kolb

Jeremy Kolb

Chicago, IL

Table of Contents

Our Free Thank You for Buying This Book

One of the recurring themes in this book is the use of specific tools to glean insight from data. This can be a confusing choice, but we welcome you to download this free report we created to break down the market leaders by strengths and weaknesses. We hope it will help you to put the ideas and techniques in this book into practice more effectively.

http://bit.ly/VZX19F

Why Data is So Critical

In 1880, a historian named Arnold Toynbee coined the phrase "industrial revolution" to describe the societal changes brought about by technology. He chose that phrase because the changes he saw were so drastic that the only similar event he could think of was the French Revolution. Today we toss the term "revolution" around a lot, but that gives you an idea of what a real revolution looks like.

Now that's what I call a revolution.

We're currently heading towards a similarly disruptive time: the Big Data Revolution.

Technological innovation has been building at a breakneck pace since the 1600 and 1700's, when a perfect storm of patent and property law, combined with the development of rudimentary capital markets, enabled inventors to spend time immersed in the development of new technologies. That bedrock of early inventions began with steam-driven coal mining pumps, coalesced into steam engines, and continues today.

The Industrial Revolution began in England with the invention of the flying shuttle and spinning jenny. In 20 years' time the amount of fiber being spun into clothing had exploded from 500,000 pounds a year to 16 MILLION pounds a year. That is quite a gain in efficiency and made the early adopters wealthy while the laggards fell far behind. Between 1875 and 1930 an astonishing number of world-changing inventions followed: the steam engine made it faster and easier to transport goods along rivers, the telephone and light bulb were invented, and the first power plants came online. The world literally changed from the Wild West into something like what we have today before the eyes of a generation.

Not coincidentally, the Industrial Revolution quite possibly saved the young American republic. During those years it experienced 6 financial panics and 4 major wars. Yet America survived this and even thrived, in large part due to the huge economic expansion brought by these immensely valuable innovations. Just after the Panic of 1873, Bell's telephone, Edison's quadruplex telegraphy, the phonograph and light bulb boosted economic activity. Around the Panic of 1893, Tesla's induction electric motor and Diesel's engine ramped up the economy again.

History doesn't repeat, it rhymes, and what we're experiencing now is mimicking the past. The United States and the world, are mired by truly staggering debt. In history only two things have happened in this situation: either the state collapses under the burden of the debt, or the society innovates its way toward exponentially faster growth.

The Internet was the last seismic shift in technology that could truly be called a revolution. This revolution began transforming our world in the 1990's, around the time President Clinton was able to ride the wave and actually pay down the national debt for the first time in generations. Since then we've only seen incremental improvements on top of that revolution.

Fortunately there is a revolution on the horizon: the Big Data Revolution. For Decades we have collected data, but until recently we never collected it in large enough quantities to even glimpse its potential, nor have we had the right idea about what to do with it. But now we *have* recently seen that potential, and a few pioneers are starting to explore it and harness the insights in it for exponential gains in efficiency, productivity, and profit.

We've been tracking this inflection point for years, and we're excited to see the tools and technology mature to the point where it's finally becoming accessible to a wider audience. This book is your guidebook—your map— telling you where you need to go and what you need to do to exploit this unique opportunity. Not at a low-level technical perspective—there are other resources for that which we will point you towards if you'd like to learn more about a specific technique—but rather from a transformational business perspective.

Data: The New Oil

One of the high level transformative aspects of data science is how it takes advantage of resources you already possess. What if I were to tell you that you had a handful of oil wells, untapped, in your backyard. You'd immediately figure out how to tap it, right?

Guess what, you probably do. They're called data sources. They're spewing real, valuable, honest-to-goodness wealth every day. And what's even better is that all that data you've been accumulating for years is actually worth something. Quite possibly a LOT of something.

Now suppose you're able to get the oil out of your back yard. You know it's worth something, but now what? Do you sell it, refine it into gasoline, or turn it into something useful like plastic? It might be attractive to sell it, but your neighbors don't know what to do with crude oil, it's not recommended for most auto models. So you'll want a refinery. No problem, just a few million bucks and you're in business.

Thankfully, extracting value from your data is much easier and less expensive than getting value from your oil. The tools are much cheaper and much more accessible. The value you are after is insight—solid, actionable, *powerful* insight.

This book will show you the techniques and tools you'll need to harness your data gushers, and gain the unique kind of advantage Procter and Gamble once had.

Why your competitors do not want you to read this book

In the 1960's Procter and Gamble was the clear market leader in baby products. And even many of its other products were advertised as baby products. Gentle laundry detergent, for example, to wash baby diapers:

During that time a P&G engineer discovered a way to use synthetic fibers from China to make a disposable baby diaper. Rather than stick this innovation in a closet somewhere, P&G decided to take the first mover advantage and create a market for disposable diapers, even at the expense of some of its other products.

Besides the fact that grocers often didn't know where to put the disposable diapers—you often saw them in food aisles at first, for example, the disposable diapers were a runaway success for P&G, and they still dominate this multi-billion dollar industry today.

There are also many examples of incumbents who fail to recognize disruptive technology or resist it to preserve existing market share. Every time disruptive technology comes along the status quo is shaken. Sometimes the major established firms in an industry use the technology to disrupt themselves, and sometimes they hold onto their existing market for dear life and then slowly watch their businesses erode until it's too late.

As you will learn in this book, data insights are truly disruptive technology. Someone in your industry will gain the first mover advantage, and potentially become the dominant force in that industry for decades.

Structure of Secrets of the Big Data Revolution

To make this as pleasant as possible to read and enjoy we've split this book into four major components:

Part 1: Data Science

In Part 1 we first introduce you to the world of data science and analytics. These are the tools companies and governments use to refine their crude data into valuable insights. In this section, we'll look at the magic behind

Amazon's success, and see how data is leading towards a near *Minority Report* future.

Part 2 Big Data

Data is growing at an exceptional rate, we produce more data now in a day than we did from the dawn of man till 2003. This explosion of data creates many unique struggles as well as opportunities. In this section we'll look at how Obama invested in Big Data during his presidential campaign and explore how startups are revealing data that saves their clients substantial capital.

Part 3 Tools of the trade

Data Scientists cannot just look at big data and get value from it, doesn't matter how good they are, the data is just too big. So companies like IBM and Microsoft build tools that help people make sense of data. The two primary categories of tools you need to be aware of are Business Intelligence and Data Discovery. In this section we explore these broad terms, and show how companies are designing more specialized tools for specific purposes.

Part 4 Gazing into the Future

In order to position yourself well for what is to come you need to know where we are now and, almost more importantly, where we are going to be in the near future. In this section we explore the trends that are going to matter as we move forward in this emerging technology industry. Computerized Data Analytics is truly still in its early stages of development, and things are going to change as new innovations come to the forefront. If we are serious about gaining the data advantage, we need to stay ahead of this curve.

Part 1: Data Science and Its Real World Applications

1.1: Data Intelligence

Before doing anything else with data, it is essential that we first understand the over-arching purpose of data analysis and the real reason for using this precious resource. It is so easy to get caught up in the buzz over data right now, and there are lots of people doing things with data just because they can. As you read this book, you need to keep one clear goal in mind: generating Data Intelligence.

Data intelligence is a broad term that describes the real, meaningful insights that can be extracted from your data—truths you can act on. The goal of any data exercise should always be to get the data intelligence out of the data.

The tech world can't stop talking about analytics, big data, data discovery, data mining, and other buzzwords and technologies. If you're not careful the hoopla will distract you—so when you hear any of these buzzwords, just think to yourself, "will that increase my data intelligence?"

The term "business intelligence" is an offshoot of this more generalized idea that specifically finds intelligence related to business operations, but has since been relegated to buzzword status as it has been overused and abused. Frankly, it is a stretch to call static reports any kind of intelligence. They are simply time-delayed answers to questions that you've already asked, and the amount of intelligence you get from them is very limited. If you're lucky they'll answer a single question you need to know the answer to, that's about it.

However, data intelligence is real and remarkably important—and whether you realize it yet or not, it's the reason you're reading this book. The insights that can be gained from data are supremely valuable as evidenced by a myriad of stories about how real companies have used intelligence gleaned from their data to transform their businesses and their industries. Here are just a few that we'll dig into more as we progress:

- Colleges are bolstering student retention rates by tailoring student experiences.

- Target is able to find and market to pregnant women with coupons simply by recognizing patterns in the products the women buy.

- Political campaigns are using data to micro target segments of the population.

The types of data intelligence required to solve a specific problem will vary. There are several different types of data intelligence—we can even put them on a scale of "Data IQ":

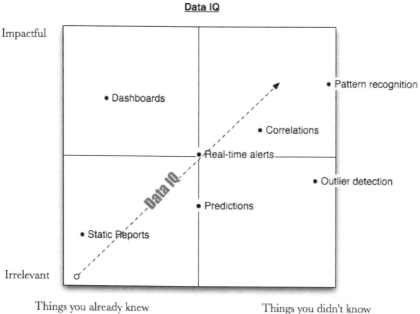

Data IQ

You get different types of information from each of these types of data intelligence:

- *Answers to questions you've already asked*—static reports fall into this category—are lowest on the Data IQ scale. Stale answers that are now inaccurate would be lower still.

- *Dashboards* display the answer to a question you've asked and updates the answer in real-time. But you have to know the right question to ask first, and they're very inflexible.

- *Outliers* can be detected and analyzed to identify opportunities and warnings. At the very least they are interesting and will give you a much better idea of what your data looks like.

- *Correlations* can be detected and reported to find key pressure points that can be manipulated to change and control trends and patterns.

- *Predictions* can be useful, but they are often limited by the data and inaccurate. If fed with the proper data, however, they can be extremely powerful.

- *Pattern recognition* is a broader term that encapsulates a few other ideas: it is usually a combination of outlier detection, correlation information, and even sometimes predictions. But they're extremely powerful, and be used to alert users to underlying movement and direction in their industry business, and customer base.

Of course, your mileage may vary depending on your specific needs, and these types of data intelligence can be combined or used alongside one another. For example pattern recognition and predictions could be incorporated into dashboards or real-time alerts.

All of these are examples of data intelligence. Right now the types of data intelligence in the upper-right quadrant of the chart are hard to get, and very complex. But as the field of business intelligence and data discovery tools matures this will quickly change and using these types of data intelligence will be a competitive necessity.

1.2: What is "Data Science"

In Russia 1770, a renowned illusionist challenged Wolfgang von Kempelen to create a machine to amaze the courtiers of his day. He accepted the challenge and created one of the greatest hoaxes of all time: The Mechanical Turk.

Using his unmatched knowledge of mechanical engineering he produced an amazing invention that appeared to have the ability to play chess: A wooden mannequin capable of grabbing and moving pieces sat behind a large wooden cabinet with a built in chessboard. When Kempelen gave demonstrations, he would open the cabinet revealing a mess of gears that looked like the inside of a clock and clearly didn't leave any room for a person underneath.

Kempelen delivered on the challenge to say the least, and took the Mechanical Turk on tour across Europe; it even played against Napoleon.

Nobody could figure out how the Turk worked, for it had a well hidden secret, within the cabinet itself there was a cramped compartment allowing one man to view the chessboard and move the mannequin above. This secret went undiscovered by many of the greatest minds of Kempelen's age and was only revealed after his death.

No matter what business you are looking to get into, you'll find that there are secrets about it insiders just don't want to reveal. Little tricks that make it seem like they are doing something truly magical, and if you don't know what's happening behind the scenes, then it is absolutely seems like magic to you. It's no different in the data industry.

Throughout this book we'll be pulling back the curtain and showing you what is really happening; showing you how companies get to those game changing insights. Clearing away the confusion so that you can better understand this fascinating industry.

One roadblock to entering, understanding, and engaging in the data industry is confusion over the meaning and scope of terms. It isn't intentional—more like the product of accumulated years of marketing buzzwords—but the confusion is there and I intend to remove it for you.

You'll notice that we keep referring to "data science" and "data scientists". These are terms that are going to come up again and again when we talk about big data and analytics, so it's worth taking a moment to break these terms down.

New territory

Data science is kind of an odd word born out of necessity that encapsulates the skills needed to refine data into insights. As we collectively started to realize the types of insights that can come from data, we needed a way to refer to the skills and processes needed to get there. It's much more awkward to say "programming, database design, and statistical analysis" than it is to say "data science".

But it's deceptive, because those skills are a sort of odd mish-mash of skills that you'll be hard pressed to find in a single person:

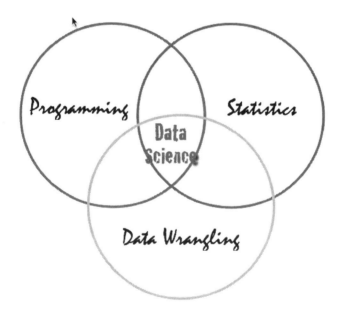

As you can see this practice known as "data science" combines three rather technical disciplines into one (data wrangling, if you haven't heard of it, is a fuzzy term which means "you know how to work with lots of data"). Which is where the analogy to the industrial revolution comes into play—data science is effectively building on technologies that were developed decades ago, recently matured, and combining them into something new and exciting.

Because of the cross-section of skills required, a company will typically hire a firm like ours that already has the necessary skill sets, or they will set up an entire data team that collectively fills this function. Consumer packages goods companies such as Proctor and Gamble, who realize they can move the needle by millions of dollars as a result of data science, have relatively large data science teams, but they're far ahead of the curve in this regard.

Proctor & Gamble Business Sphere

Just to give you an idea of the level of sophistication we're talking about when we look at companies that have dedicated data science teams, the above picture is of a room at Proctor and Gamble dedicated purely to viewing and understanding data. This book is focused on companies that aren't at that level of sophistication... yet.

Our goal is to level the playing field somewhat by teaching you the right questions to ask and how to get those questions answered.

Data Science

Data Science is the umbrella term for everything within the data industry. So if someone uses the term, they are either referring to the collective data industry, or they are looking at any one part of it and simply using the umbrella term. In this book, the term Data Science will only be used as the umbrella term it is. So let's define it.

In order to build a solid understanding of what people mean by data science, it is worthwhile to look at the term from a few different angles so you can build a complete framework for it. First let's consider the data science process.

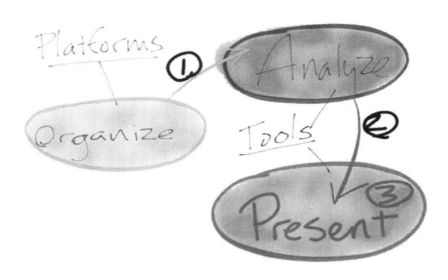

From a technical standpoint, Data Science primarily involves three things: organizing, analyzing, and presenting data.

Organizing Data is often referred to as "data warehousing" and is the process of cleaning, joining, and storing data so that it can be properly analyzed. In Section 2.3 we'll look at how the 2012 Obama Campaign organized their data, a move credited for earning Obama over half a million votes according to some pundits. In Section 2.4 we'll look at some technologies used to organize large amounts of data, and in Section 2.5 we'll see how IBM is using the *Jeopardy!* playing Watson technology to treat cancer.

Analyzing Data, or simply "analytics", involves using techniques like clustering, predictive modeling, pattern recognition, and outlier detection among others to reveal insights about your business that can increase profits, reduce costs, reveal hidden opportunities, and improve efficiency. This crosses into the statistical analysis side of data science, but it gets much more difficult because of the amount of data you're working with. These techniques are the kind that make news, like when Target revealed their pregnancy prediction algorithm which we'll talk about in section 1.4, or in section 1.6 how Amazon schooled the world with what could be done with online shopping data.

Presenting Data is where traditional business intelligence tools, infographics and data visualizations come into play. In section 3.1 we'll discuss these tools in more detail. Presenting data is the final step in this process, and if it isn't done in a way that builds understanding, then the whole process is a failure.

Organizing, analyzing, and presenting data are all part of the data science process, a process that reveals hidden correlations and patterns within data that provide better understanding of the subject being studied. This ability, the ability to take data, organize, understand, and communicate it, is becoming extremely valuable in our society and the value is only going up.

What is a Data Scientist?

Not long ago, I was talking to a group of high school students, teaching them about entrepreneurship and the changes coming because of the digital age. One of the kids asked the question: "If you were in my shoes, what would you want to be after college?"

Of course I answered, "A Data Scientist. There really aren't enough good ones, and the demand for them just keeps going up... Oh, and it's a hell of a lot of fun."

A good data scientist needs to be well versed in statistics and mathematics, have a working knowledge of computer programming, and have a good amount of experience dealing with data. Although we're going to be exploring the business side of Data Science, it is worth noting that the best data scientists are often those with backgrounds in the "hard sciences" *as well as experience in the business*. Proficiency in these core skills along with an understanding of their industry allows data scientists to tap the value hidden in data. By merging data resources, ensuring consistency of data sets, interpreting data through analytics, and creating visualizations to aid in understanding, data scientists are changing the way we see the world.

One notable data scientist is Hans Rosling, a statistician, medical doctor, and Professor of International Health at Karolinka Insitute.

Professor Rosling's famous TED talks and videos clearly demonstrate the power of data and how it can change the world.

To produce his presentations, Dr. Rosling has to practice all the things listed above. For the presentation on world health, he merges datasets from governments all over the world, ensures consistency, makes the data work together, uses analytics to determine the appropriate variables, and finally creates a visualization that changes your mind. Dr. Rosling and his team do all this masterfully, and the end result is a wonderful example of what a data scientist is and what they do.

The ins and outs of Data Science

The final way we're going to look at Data Science is by breaking it down into its parts and looking at where they fit in the process. Data Science is the process of taking raw data, producing information from that data, and using that information to build understanding.

Data is any collection of numbers, text, audio, video; essentially any raw binary input that can be processed by a computer. This data is then collected, and unified—a process which we will discuss in more detail in Section 2.3. To make the data science process clear, I'm going to use a grocery store as our example. When it comes to data, you'll find that consumer-oriented companies have a *lot* of it. They have data about each customers' purchasing habits, overall inventory, pricing, sales, etc. All this data is used to get to the next component of this process: *Information*.

Information is gained by understanding the underlying patterns and correlations in the data. It is what is left after you sift the noise from a data set.

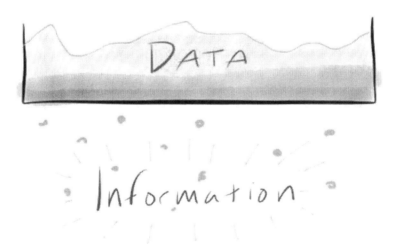

By itself data is a worthless collection of 0's and 1's, but by building connections that provide context, we can start to tease out correlations and patterns. These correlations and patterns present initial insights, which trigger questions. **Data only becomes valuable when you can gain information from it, and it becomes information when it starts answering the questions of who, what, where, when, and how**. For Example, let's say our grocery store has decided to jump on the Big Data train and has started analyzing their sales data. In the process they found an improbable and crazy correlation: a regular pattern of increased beer and diaper sales on Thursdays. Now they have a bit of information and can move on to the final step: taking that data and making it into usable knowledge or *understanding*.

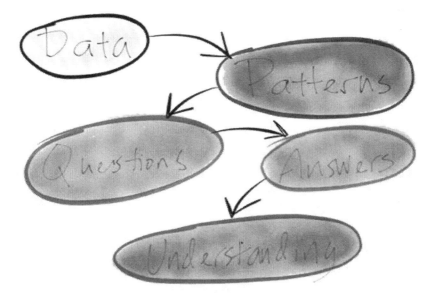

Understanding comes when information enables the forecasting and utilization of data to produce positive outcomes. Instead of just knowing what and where, you can identify why a particular thing is happening and take advantage of it. The grocery store data science team identifies that this increase in beer and diaper sales is connected to young fathers getting ready for the weekend. The sales team then placed chips and other snacks in the aisle between the diapers and beer, and as a result, snack sales increase on Thursdays. This is a good example of understanding; the data science team used the data to find information and understanding in order to drive snack sales.

1.3: Overview of the Data Pipeline

In section 1.4 we're going to talk about how Target uses data to learn their customers' secrets, but before we do that, we need to take a detour to explain some fundamentals.

The technical side of Data Science can be a bit daunting, but in order to understand why and how things work you need to have a cursory understanding of the process. So let's take a short look at your typical data pipeline.

A data pipeline is what happens to your data from the time it's generated to the time you see information on a screen somewhere. In between those two points a whole lot can and usually does happen, including the implementation of the various algorithms that we'll be covering. This process typically starts with data warehousing.

The core process of data warehousing is called Extract, Transform, Load (ETL), and is core to Data Science.

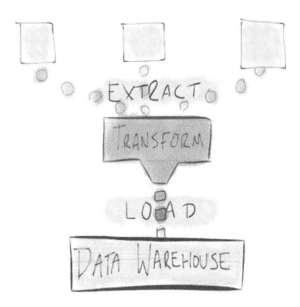

The data warehousing process takes data from multiple sources (extract), cleans and transforms it into a uniform structure (transform), and stores the now uniform data (load).

Extraction Stage

Extraction is the first step, and in it the data is taken from each of the data sources and merged. This isn't always as easy as it sounds.

I was recently working with data for a Fortune 100 business-to-business company. Their customer interaction data is spread across several different systems: billing, customer service, and operations. In order to get any kind of information that crosses these functional boundaries this data had to be integrated together so that we could get a complete view of their interactions with their customers.

The problem was that there was no "conversation identifier" that was common across systems, so there was no way to tie a billing question in with a subsequent payment and follow-up call. The conversation turned into series of disjointed communiqués as far as the data could tell.

This is actually a very common problem, and one you're likely to run into if you're operating in a large organization. Data often simply isn't in an ideal state. This is also where some of the data science magic comes in, and these are the kinds of problems that makes data scientists their bread and butter. To get around this we did some manual classification to provide the system with some training examples that it then used to automagically determine when multiple interactions were part of the same conversation. This type of an approach is not 100% accurate but it's accurate enough to be useful for extracting statistically valid insights.

In data science there are times when there is no "right" answer, it's more like a series of tricks and black magic that need to be performed in order to get the system functioning "right enough". **If there are fundamental system problems, data science can be used to duct tape together a solution,**

sometimes covering up the underlying issues. It's not ideal, but it can create value quickly while you work on a long-term solution.

In any case, the extracted data can end up in a few different places:

- It's common to extract data to a .CSV (comma-separated value) file so that it can be sent somewhere else via email, FTP and so on.
- Sometimes entire data is kept in native database format, or simply stored in memory, to be sent through the next steps in the ETL process.
- Occasionally you will see other formats, such as Excel files, although this is somewhat uncommon.

The extracted data, whatever the resulting storage format, is then sent on to the next stage for transformation.

Transformation stage

The transformation stage has three steps: cleansing, normalization, and analysis.

Transformation Step 1: Cleansing

A big part of this process is cleaning your data. Data is most often entered or recorded by people, and people make mistakes. Duplicate records are among the most common errors and are one a lot of us have experience with; for most things these kinds of errors are simply annoying, but when you're analyzing data they can lead to screwy results.

The purity of the input data is going to depend on the system it's coming from. Most newer enterprise-grade systems do a decent job of keeping the data clean, but there are still many data sources that aren't as friendly.

Take for example a point-of-sale system where the cashier is required to type in the customer's name. A modern system will assist the cashier if she types "SIMTH" instead of "SMITH", but older systems with no built-in protection mechanisms won't. And so it's up to the ETL process to realize that "JANE SIMTH" in the point of sale system is the same as "JANE SMITH" in the customer loyalty database.

Cleansing also takes care of removing obviously wrong data, such as text in a dollar amount field and so on.

Transformation Step 2: Normalization

Normalization is the act of turning records from different sources into a common format. This step is needed because it's remarkably rare for different data sources to share the same underlying format.

For example, a customer relationship management system may contain a customer record in the following format:

Name	State	Gender
Jane Smith	IL	Female

While your sales management system contains the exact same record, but in a different format:

Name	State	Gender
Jane Smith	Illinois	F

Normalization is the process of turning these two records into a common definitive—and most importantly **consistent**—format so that all of the resulting analysis will correctly recognize these records as talking about the same customer rather than two different customers.

Transformation Step 3: Analysis

During the warehousing process, data is often analyzed. Traditionally this has been very rudimentary, including such items as "rolling up" or "summarizing data". This is merely the process of taking individual transactions in the data and summarizing, them, often to a specific time period such as a day:

Date	Customer	Quantity	Total Order
January 12	John Doe	5	$100
January 12	Jane Doe	1	$20

Transactions (not yet rolled up)

Date	Quantity	Total Order
January 12	6	$120

Summarized transactions for a single day

These "rollups" or summaries are the data that goes into traditional business intelligence applications and dashboards. So-called because they roll up multiple records into a single record. But we're interested in applications a little more sophisticated than that. One of the exciting ways data is analyzed is through the use of algorithms.

Simply put an algorithm is a set of rules a computer follows in order to perform an action. For example in Section 1.6 we'll see how Amazon uses recommender algorithms to increase sales.

Many of the algorithms we'll talk about fall into the category of Data Mining. Data Mining is a specific subset of analytics that does some very cool things like pattern recognition, predictions, and classifications. We'll talk about some of these techniques throughout the book, but you need to know that data mining is often done as part of the ETL process as well.

Some data mining algorithms, specifically those called Machine Learning algorithms, use a set of known good data called training data to learn what you need to predict. For example you can feed a machine learning algorithm a set of tweets that are already labeled as positive or negative sentiment-wise, and the algorithm will learn characteristics of what indicates a positive or negative tweet. You'll usually create the training set using human beings, and then the algorithm essentially learns and copies their behavior. This is often used for sentiment analysis which we cover in section 2.5 and spam filtering.

Data mining is typically done during this stage as well. The newly transformed and ready-for-storage data is sent to machine learning algorithms to generate models, predictions, classifications, and so on.

A note about analysis

The Analysis step of the Transform stage is where much of the Data Science magic happens. Once the data is made to be uniform and can cooperatively work together (traditionally this is called "normalized" data), the algorithms can be applied to it to create brand new data—the end product of the algorithms. As we'll talk more about in section 1.7, you can think of the algorithms themselves as a brand new source of data: they take the raw data from the original data sources and create new, refined data out of it. And in fact you can even keep going from there: you can combine the output of the algorithms with original data, or even output from other algorithms, and snowball that into even more meaningful pools of data.

Load stage

The load is a relatively simple step – it is the act of loading your data into the data warehouse. It could easily be called storage. The only caveat to this is that ETL processes can be strung together—the output from one ETL process can be loaded into another ETL process, acting as a data extraction source.

The ultimate location of the data being stored will depend on the toolset you end up using, but it's typically a very heavy-duty relational or noSQL database (we'll cover these terms in the Big Data section).

Data Inventory and filling gaps

Any well-run warehouse conducts inventories, and data warehouses are no different. In fact, the first and most important inventory should happen before the data warehouse is built because knowing what you have helps you know what you can do; it's the foundation of every Big Data project.

A data inventory is a catalogue of available and applicable data. The data inventory is built by exploring both internal data and external data. Once this is built, you need to decide what data sources need to be pulled into the data warehouse.

One of the most difficult parts of establishing a data project is figuring out what data is needed for success. Typically it's not even considered—it's simply "this is the data we have to work with". But this is one of the key points that separates the professionals from the amateurs in this field: professionals know how to fill the data gaps.

To do this you'll need to know:

1. What data is available (the objects and properties—or fields and tables—that are in the data)
2. What form the data is currently in (is it available in a database? As an export from a product? Via connecting to an API?)
3. How often you get fresh data (An API will typically give fresh data, while an export might only get updated once a day)

If you realize your data isn't sufficient, then what you have is an Information Gap. This gap is the difference between what data you have and what data you need. After identifying this gap, you then have to determine how much of the gap needs to be filled from internal sources and how much can be filled externally.

There are many sources of external data you can use to plug information gaps. Here are a few to get you going:

- Infochimps is perhaps the leading data marketplace, offering data on everything from Twitter to energy consumption.

- Microsoft Azure Data Market offers many different types of data including real estate, transportation, consumer goods, and many more.
- Pew Research, the famous survey-taking company that is often quoted on the news, offers many of its data sets for download and use.

There are many other data markets, but this should be enough to get you started.

Once all the data you need is gathered it needs to be integrated into a Data Warehouse. Data warehouse projects aren't cheap—they can often run into the hundreds of thousands of dollars—so be sure you need it. You may want to talk to a data consultant to help understand the scope of what you're looking at.

Now we'll take a look at how Target used an algorithm in a unique way to create customers for a lifetime.

Section 1.4: Learning Customer Secrets

At a Target outside of Minneapolis an angry father burst in demanding to talk with the manager. He was clutching a mailer sent to his teenage daughter. He didn't understand how Target could be so immoral as to send teenage girls ads for baby clothes and cribs. "Are you encouraging her to get pregnant?!" he indignantly asked. The manager looked at the mailer and quickly understood the father's anger. Cute babies and pregnant mothers on the cover of an ad with coupons for maternity clothes and baby formula. The manager apologized profusely and assured the father he would look into it personally and it would not happen again.

One of the offers the daughter received

A few days later the manager called the father to apologize again for the company's error, but instead it was the fathers turn to say he was sorry. "It turns out there's been some activities in my house I haven't been completely aware of. She's due in August. I owe you an apology."

Statisticians get asked some weird questions, and for Target's Andrew Pole, his came from marketing: "If we wanted to figure out if a customer is pregnant, even if she didn't want us to know, can you do that?"

What? Why would they want to know that?

And this is where it gets really interesting, and where conventional psychology plays into the data mining process. People build habitual lives, they go to the same places, shop at the same stores, and build comfortable routines for themselves. It's hard to change these life patterns; to get people to start shopping at your store and stop going to that other one. But psychologists have discovered that there are certain times in a person's life when these patterns are more susceptible to alteration, big life changes like becoming pregnant trigger these susceptible times.

Ever since marketers learned of this, they've been trying to target customers before, during, and after these experiences, and companies like Target are fighting over these customers to try to gain any advantage they can. That's why Pole came up with the "Pregnancy Prediction" so Target might know a few weeks before their competition that a mother is expecting.

If Target could find these customers during this period of flux, they had an opportunity to capture them for the rest of their lives.

"We knew that if we could identify mothers in their second trimester, there's a good chance we could capture them for years," said Pole. "As soon as we get them buying diapers from us, they're going to start buying everything else too. If you're rushing through the store, looking for bottles, and you pass orange juice, you'll grab a carton. Oh, and there's that new DVD I want. Soon, you'll be buying cereal and paper towels from us, and keep coming back."

So Pole and his team got to work, mining through vast data warehouses and public records. They explored past records of customers known to have had a child and looked for purchasing trends among them that could predict pregnancy. Soon the patterns emerged. Unscented lotions and soaps, cotton balls, zinc and magnesium supplements, and vitamins, these are among the 25 products Pole used to build a predictable pattern expecting mothers would follow. These products formed the basis for Targets "Pregnancy Prediction", a prediction providing a pregnancy percentage likelihood that even estimates a mother's due date.

Soon after this was built, Target started sending ads based on expected due date.

This Data Science project was wildly successful for Target. Minus a few hiccups like the teenager in Minneapolis. It turns out pregnant women, much like all of us, don't like the feeling of being spied on so Target made some changes to its program to avoid the creepiness factor. They found out that if they added innocuous items such as laundry soap next to the pregnancy sales people didn't feel as targeted. They just added a touch of randomness to the mailers. With wineglass coupons next to vitamin supplements and garage door openers next to baby diapers, Target stopped creeping out customers and started winning loyalty.

How it Works
Target is a company that knows the value of continually enriching data, and that's how they're able to pull off tricks like identifying pregnant women by their buying patterns. Target maintains a database of customers, and if you've ever shopped at Target you're in it. It keeps a list of each credit card and email address a customer uses, and a complete list of purchases they've ever made. Since they maintain this customer record and complete history, and they can also track when women sign up for a gift registry for a baby shower, they have a fairly accurate indication of changing buying patterns leading up to a woman registering for baby gifts.

Pole was able to identify about 25 products that, when analyzed together, allowed him to assign each shopper a "pregnancy prediction" score. More important, he could also estimate her due date to within a small window, so Target could send coupons timed to very specific stages of her pregnancy.

For example imagine a woman that suddenly buys cocoa-butter lotion, a purse large enough to double as a diaper bag, zinc and magnesium supplements and a bright blue rug. That information can be used to assign a prediction score of say, 75 to the chance that she's pregnant, and you can guess fairly accurately when she's due within a month or two of those purchases.

How to Do it

There are a few ways to obtain this sort of insight from data. One is trial and error, having a data scientist do a manual classification exercise where he looks at known cases of pregnant customers and attempts to divine patterns from them, testing hypotheses against known good data. However, this approach is very manual, doesn't scale well, and notably requires a data scientist.

Another approach uses what is called a Sequence Clustering Algorithm, which is an algorithm that attempts to find common paths, or sequences, which lead to specific events. Typically these algorithms are run against time-based event data, such as buying habits. Other data sets that are great candidates for sequence clustering algorithms include:

> Click paths that are created when users navigate or browse a Website.
>
> Logs that list events preceding an incident, such as hard disk failure or server deadlocks.
>
> Records that follow customer (or patient) interactions over time, to predict service cancellations or other poor outcomes.

Sequence Clustering Algorithms vary in their implementations, but almost all of them use some variation of Markov Chain Analysis (which you can learn more about on our resource page or in appendix A). Markov chains are used to determine the probabilities of something moving from one state to another by using a set of training data and determining the distances (using distance calculations, which we will look at in section 1.6) between all possible sequences, and using those distances to determine the sequences that best represent real-world buying patterns for similar customers (or click paths, or log events, or interactions, etc).

JARGON WATCH

"Training data" is data with some known properties—specifically, you know that it contains examples of the outcome you are looking for. Not all algorithms require training data, but the ones that do learn how to act by trying to extract rules from the training data that you give them—these rules are then called a "model".

Markov chains are interesting algorithms useful for many different things in computer science. They essentially analyze and predict the probability that something will go from one state to another. For example, they are sometimes used to create computer-generated text by calculating the most probable word to follow another, or to follow the previous sequence of words. This results in often entertaining computer-generated gobbledygook such as the following:

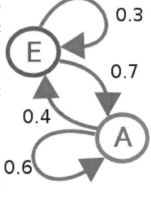

A Markov Chain

> **Can you put a few years of your twin-brother Alfred, who was apt to rally round a bit. I should strongly advocate the blue with milk.**

This text was generated by doing a Markov chain analysis of *My Man Jeeves* by Wodehouse: you can see that while it is complete nonsense it is also somewhat coherent nonsense, and if you're familiar with *My Man Jeeves*, you can see how this sentence might come from rules generated by analyzing that book. It doesn't understand the meaning of each step in the chain, but it does a decent job of stringing together links that might conceivably come after one another.

CUSTOMER ANALYTICS
BLUEPRINT

If you'd like more information about the steps to take to drive specific behaviors, we'd love to share that with you. To get our FREE **Customer Analytics Blueprint**,

Click here to get it

http://bit.ly/14smRH4

Section 1.5: Playing Precog

If you're a parolee in Maryland or Pennsylvania and you're thinking about killing someone, you'd better keep an eye out for the police. There's a decent chance they've already identified you as a potential problem and are watching closely. Like many companies, the justice departments of Maryland and Pennsylvania are investing in data and using predictive analytics.

In one of the those great examples of science fiction foreshadowing reality, the movie *Minority Report* used predictive technology for crime fighting, and we're now seeing that play out all over the world. *Minority Report* focuses on a future where murders are prevented by knowing who, what, where, and when a crime is going to take place. Three characters called precogs prophetically know about murders, and an agency tasked with interpreting their visions arrests the soon to be murderers before they kill their victims.

While we don't yet have precogs, patterns in data give us real insight into what, when, and where something is likely to happen. When *Minority Report* hit theaters in 2002, data and analytics were not nearly as powerful as they are now, and using data to prevent crime seemed like an impossible dream. However, times have changed and now a few tech savvy cities are showing us glimpses of what might be possible. We're now in a place where we can take the ideas of *Minority Report* and replace the psychic aspect with real and proven big data-driven technology.

Several of California's large cities are leading the way in the Big Data world and San Francisco is one of them. It is one of many cities with wide open data; everything from crime to housing is freely available and Data Science teams are creating transformative tools with this wealth of information.

Exploring the tools these teams created allows us a glimpse into the possible future of the data driven city; a future where data drives funding and planning. Right now most cities grossly ignore the wealth of information they store. A company called Stamen is trying to exploit that wealth of insight, and they have built an intriguing tool to do just that called CrimeSpotting.

CrimeSpotting is a Web site created by Stamen that provides a truly unique and fun way to explore crime data. The program shows crime stats on an interactive map that allows you to filter based on time of day, type of crime, and time of year among others. Currently this tool only serves to report on what happened and isn't being used preventively by San Francisco police, but it's a step in the right direction.

Interestingly, there are police departments out there that actually *are* doing prevention using data, today.

Beyond Spotting: to preventing

Police in Maryland and Pennsylvania are taking an even more data science-driven approach. They are crunching databases of tens of thousands of crimes and looking for patterns. Those patterns help police reduce crime by predicting when crimes are likely to occur, and who's likely to commit them. The software they've developed automates the decisions that were once made by police officers and judges, and this move to data-based decision making has dramatically decreased the percentage of repeat offenders among parolees.

Now this isn't exactly like the precogs from *Minority Report*, but it might be closer than you think. With the data and analytics, a department can receive a daily report of possible crimes including likelihood, location, and timeframe, all with ranges and calculated probability. With this type of knowledge, a department can make better decisions about where to deploy resources, and they could truly be in the business of crime prevention.

This is just one way government could use data and analytics to make society safer, and the wealth of data available to the government is staggering. If cities start using data to its full potential, those pristine cities from Sci-Fi movies won't seem as far-fetched as they do now.

How it Works

Maryland and Pennsylvania assembled over 60,000 crime records with dozens of different variables and used it to decide which factors were the best predictors of behaviors. It turns out that the age at which the person committed their crime and the type of crime were far and away the best indicators in their data set.

"People assume that if someone murdered once then they will murder in the future," said Richard Berk, the developer of the software. "But what really matters is what that person did as a young individual. If they committed armed robbery at age 14 that's a good predictor. If they committed the same crime at age 30, that doesn't predict very much."

While this doesn't approach the futuristic capabilities of the precogs in *Minority Report* it does provide a useful case study if you're interested in using your data to make predictions as well. It illustrates several of the key steps required if you wish to do similar tricks with your data.

How to Do It

As noted, the linchpin in the ability of these police departments' ability to effectively predict murders was their identification of *what they should be looking at.* In this case, the person's age and type of crime—but it will be different of course for each application. Much of data science revolves around this key problem: given mountains of data, what should you be paying attention to?

What Question Should I Be Asking?

A recurring theme throughout this book is the importance of knowing the right question to ask. If you think back to our Data IQ chart, knowing the question you should be asking is typically found in the upper-right quadrant: Thing You Didn't Know, that are Impactful.

There are a few different tools in the data science toolbox that are typically used to help figure out which question you should be asking:

Exploratory factor analysis

Principal component analysis

Other more novel approaches, such as spectral analysis

Most of these techniques revolve around computing the correlation between different variables—that is, how often two variables move together, or move apart. This is done using something called a covariance matrix, which tells you how related each variable is to every other variable. The values range from -1 (perfect negative correlation) to +1 (perfect positive correlation), with 0 being no correlation at all. Positive correlations mean that the two variables move in lockstep, negative correlations mean they move in opposite directions. For example weight is often very positively correlated with height, because people who are taller tend to weigh more. But this isn't a perfect correlation because there are short heavy people and tall light people.

Most statistical packages can calculate these numbers for you. If you want to go any deeper you'll start getting into more esoteric topics such as eigenvectors. If you'd like to dig deeper into that type of analytics, you can find great resources on the topic on our resources page.

Exploratory Factor Analysis

The algorithms you use depend on your needs: exploratory factor analysis is a popular technique for determining which variables in a set of data actually matter for the sake of whatever you're trying to discover.

The one critique of exploratory factor analysis is that it assumes that there's always some underlying cause, even when there may not be. This can lead you to chase false statistical causes, and because of that it can also make you question legitimate causes.

Principal Component Analysis

Principal component analysis is similar to exploratory factor analysis but is at its core a *dimension reduction* technique. That's data science-speak for saying that it reduces the number of things you have to look at down to only those that actually matter. It is capable of combining multiple underlying factors that drive the same outcome into "merged" factors, but you must know in advance how many of those "merged" factors you need at the end of the process. This is a shortcoming of the technique because it means you often have to play with the output, manually tweaking the number of principal components you're looking for, before the output makes sense.

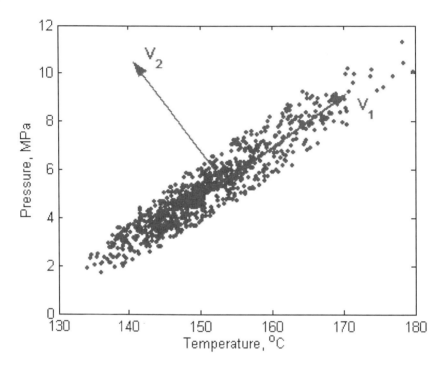

Presented in graphical terms, Principle Component Analysis plots the data in multiple dimensions, and find the largest possible variance—v1 in the picture above

As you can imagine the formulas behind things like that can get complex—but that's ok. As long as you understand the idea of it you can find the right tools and/or people to help you realize your data vision.

Spectral Analysis and Others

There are other types of root cause analysis algorithms that are starting to come into vogue for various reasons. For example spectral analysis explores data using techniques originally developed for sound and energy analysis, and has the advantage of not needing to know in advance how many groups of entities ultimately need to be found.

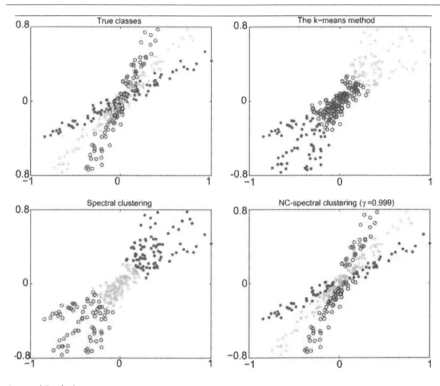

Spectral Analysis

Sometimes the tools you use for your data analysis will have these algorithms available, but most of the tools don't. If you're interested in these advanced algorithms feel free to subscribe to our mailing list (http://bit.ly/XGa8fV) where we regularly report on such topics.

Section 1.6: Sales Analytics

In 1994, a scrappy little online store entered the crowded bookseller market. A guy named Jeff Bezos started Amazon.com in his garage with a vision of what the online commerce market could become, and he realized data was the key.

I ordered it Prime!

Bezos wanted to change the way we shop by using a data-driven approach, and he was constantly told it wouldn't work. It's hard to think of what the world was like before Amazon, before online shopping transformed our economy. But back then, the idea that people would buy something without first holding it in their hands sounded ridiculous. But Bezos understood the value of data, and used it to turn his dream into reality.

When Amazon entered the bookselling business, Borders and Barnes & Noble owned the market; stores all across the nation and solid revenues made them the giants of the industry. But Bezos realized online retailers were going to have an advantage over their brick and mortar competitors, a secret if you will. Borders and Barnes & Noble were invincible in the standard market, but they had only one location to gather data from their customers: the register. Compared to the data collection abilities of an online retailer transaction data is nothing.

If you've used Google Analytics at all, you know a little about the data advantage Amazon had that Borders could only dream about. Amazon knows not only what you purchase, but what you look at, how long you look at it, what you look at next, and much more. When it comes to tailoring a user's experience, big box stores cannot compete with what online retailers have to offer.

The hurdle Amazon had to conquer was how to turn all this data into value, and they succeed in splendid fashion. Bezos slew the industry giants; Barnes and Noble now trails far behind Amazon, and Borders went bankrupt.

In 1999, Bezos was named "Time Magazine's Person of the Year" for proving online shopping was not only a solid business model but the way of the future. In 2001, Amazon recorded its first profit and hasn't looked back since.

The trick behind Amazon's mercurial growth was their data. They were one of the first companies to recognize the value in their data and they exploited it faster than anyone else. Bezos specifically realized the value in the shopping history data that nobody else was using at the time (except to show order history for returns, customer service, etc.) He knew that in that data was invaluable information about how, why, and what people purchased, and that what people purchased told a story about what other things they would likely purchase as well.

How it Works

This nifty trick works using a process called a *Recommender Algorithm* also known as *Basket Analysis*, or *Affinity Analysis*. These algorithms don't know what it feels like to read a good book, and don't prefer one subject over another. All they know is that people who bought Book A also bought Book B, and people who rated Book B highly also rate Book C highly. It's ultimately very simple data, but out of this elemental stuff something interesting can emerge if you set it up correctly and give it enough data.

 **Recommended** for You

Amazon.com has new recommendations for you based on items you purchased or told us you own.

| The Little Big Things: 163 Ways to Pursue EXCELLENCE | Fascinate: Your 7 Triggers to Persuasion and Captivation | Sherlock Holmes [Blu-ray] | Alice in Wonderland [Blu-ray] |

The reason we're talking about this is because it clearly demonstrates the value that you can get from these secrets: a cold, hard algorithm can distill elemental data into something that feels personal somehow; it engages the user in a way that only a human should be able to, but on a much larger scale.

How to Do It

Recommendation systems can, of course, be used for a much wider range of purposes than suggesting products for people to buy. And they regularly are, for purposes as diverse as recommending interesting articles online to recommending possible friends on Facebook. And in fact it is our hope that as you read this book you can take the principles behind these techniques and apply to them to new areas in ways that we've never even thought of before

The simplest recommender systems typically start by finding sets of customers with overlapping purchases and item ratings. The algorithm then eliminates items that the user has already purchased or rated and recommends the remaining items.

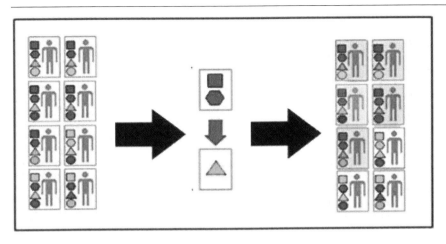

That guy clearly needs a green triangle

The other approach is to find items that are similar to other items and recommend those. In this case you are not focusing on the similarities between *customers* so much as you are comparing the similarities between *products.* Inside sources indicate that this is the approach that Amazon takes for the simple reason that they have fewer items than users, which makes this approach more scalable for them.

So as you can see, no matter which way you go the most complex part of this whole deal is finding things that are similar to other things. And this is the only part of this trick that involves anything complex at all, because the way you find similar things will affect your success with this trick.

Measuring Distance

"Distance" is something you'll see quite a lot in data science algorithms. This can sound very intimidating in a math-y kind of way, but all it really means is that if you break something into a number of properties or traits, you could consider each one of those a dimension. A dishwasher has data dimensions describing how many gallons of water it uses, how many plates it can fit, and what kind of display and buttons it uses. You can generally boil down a description of anything into a bunch of dimensions. [1]

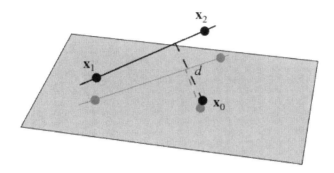

When we talk about measuring distance between data points (such as dishwashers) we're talking about the distance between points on multiple dimensions. This is easy when you're dealing with two dimensions, like you would on piece of paper--it's basic geometry. And it's a little harder to grasp, but still not too bad, when working in three dimensions, because we spend our day in three dimensions and so it's easy to visualize the distance between things in three dimensions. But when you deal with a product being represented in, say, 10 dimensions, it gets a whole lot harder to comprehend. But it's really not important that you're able to figure this out in your head because fortunately computers are very good at it. As long as you understand that distance is ultimately just a way to describe how close—or similar—two things are, you'll be fine.

How to Do It Really Well
One of the key themes that you'll see over and over in this book is that more data leads to more options, and ultimately more powerful insights.

Over the years Amazon has added many other data sources to its algorithm, making it increasingly relevant and powerful:

---

[1] http://mathworld.wolfram.com/Point-LineDistance3-Dimensional.html

They can consider items that people added to their cart but later abandoned.

They can run experiments packaging multiple products together to see how they sell together.

They can watch people's wish lists to find aspirational items.

They can observe how long you spend looking at different items

They know where you live and can combine demographic data with your buying behavior.

In fact, one of the real secrets to revolutionary data science is knowing which pieces of data matter for any given decision. And sometimes, just sometimes, you can discern what those are by watching ultra-successful data-driven companies and reading between the lines, so to speak. Each time Amazon adds another piece of data to the secret mix they have yet another dimension to measure you on and refine the algorithm that feeds you recommendations.

Amazon is the master at this, and it's always wise to learn from people who know more about something than you. We would all be wise to pay attention to what Amazon's doing, and try to figure out what the reason is for each thing they show on their page. One thing you can be sure of with Amazon is that they are 100% driven by data, so if you see something on their site there's a reason for it.

SALES ANALYTICS
BLUEPRINT

Sales analytics is a fascinating topic with lots of different nuances. If you'd like to learn more about it, we'd like to share a FREE **Sales Analytics Blueprint**,

Click here to get it

http://bit.ly/164luxZ

Section 1.7: Customer Retention

The U.S. higher education system has a problem: students are dropping out at increasing rates. Over a third of all students drop out before completing their degrees and only half complete a 4 year bachelor's. In other words, colleges are failing to keep their students, and educators are scrambling for answers. Some forward-thinking institutions are asking, "can data analytics help?" Rio Salado Community College thinks so, and their innovative solutions have applications that reach beyond education.

Statistics of the
COLLEGE DROP-OUT

3 million STUDENTS enroll in some form of higher education **each year**

33%
of students **dropped out** of college

40%
will not get a degree

53%
of students at **public institutions** drop out

38%
of students graduate within **six years**

25%
leaving college are **Freshman**

64%
of students going to a **non-profit** drop out

56%
earn a **bachelor's degree**

Top 20 Reasons for
DROPPING OUT

1 Finances
38% of students

2 Failing
28% of students

3 Outside Job
71% of students

4 Unprepared

5 Partying

6 Wrong course

7 Bad Fit
13% of students

8 Family Problems

9 Bad love

10 Homesick

11 No Mentor

12 Health
5% of students

13 New Course

14 Life

15 Move

16 Children

17 Distance
4% of students

18 Housing

19 Outside Problems

20 Burn Out
21% of students

CLASSES:CAREERS

This topic has far-reaching implications because it touches on one of the holy grails of business: customer retention. It's well known that it costs about five times as much to get a new customer (customer acquisition) as it does to retain existing customers (customer acquisition), so this is a hot-button across just about every industry.

For any college, losing students is a problem, but for Arizona's Rio Salado it's even worse. Rio Salado is primarily an online university, which means that dropout barriers are minimal, and their target market is high risk students who are mostly poor and first-generation U.S. citizens. It's a risky plan, but by using data driven solutions Rio Salado is beating the odds and juicing their bottom line while helping students better their lives. In many cases it's just a matter of giving students support at the right times so they don't get discouraged and give up.

Rio Salado has taken a page from Amazon's playbook: If you're a student at Rio Salado, all your data is being recorded; when you log on, when you log off, what you view (or don't), how long you're on the site, and so on. These metrics are used to build a data-based profile about you and determine the probability you'll pass your class and graduate.

"In some ways, it's kind of to be expected if you look at online courses as a parallel to in-person courses," said dean of Instructional Design Michael Cottam. "If students show up, participate and do pretty well on the assignments, they'll be successful. But the difference is that now we have data that's tracked every day on what a student does in a course."

It turns out that 8 days of data is all it takes to predict the likelihood a student will successfully complete their class. After 8 days, students are divided into three risk levels and monitored for changes from that point on. Armed with this data, the faculty can focus their attention on helping those at risk of failing. Some of this is automated, text messages about unfinished assignments and discussions they haven't yet contributed to, but the personal touch is heavily relied upon to pull those students back into the class.

"We wanted to be able to identify at-risk students early because the earlier in a course you can predict whether a student is going to be at risk, the more time you have to put interventions in place—support structures, contacts, and so on that could help mitigate the risk."

This predictive analytics solution is still in the testing phase, but so far Rio Salado has raised their retention rate for online classes to 68% a full 18% higher than the national average.

Interest in data mining and predictive analytics is a growing focus of higher education, and Rio Salado is just one example. Their student retention parallels what many other companies are trying to do with customer retention in many other industries.

How it works

Return customers are the bread and butter for all businesses: the Pareto Principle applied here says that 80% of your sales come from 20% of your clients. The goal of customer retention analytics is to make sure you do whatever you can to make that 20% happy and give them what they need to succeed. Enable your best customers. At the same time, it's very probable that 20% of your customers are eating 80% of your costs, which means you'll want to make sure that it's worth it to spend your limited resources making those customers happy.

In order to improve their student retention rates, Rio Salado used two common data science techniques: Segmentation/Clustering and Predictive Modeling.

Customer Segmentation

Rio Salado is currently optimizing their student retention through extensive and focused testing, and they're finding some truly telling results. But because they're a college, they automatically have some data other businesses have to work to discover: their customers come segmented and customer goals are explicit.

One of the challenges most companies will face when doing customer analysis like this is to break their customer base down into logical groups who either behave similarly or have a common set of desires or needs. Most companies will need to employ techniques like the ones we talked about in Section 1.5 (Principal Component Analysis, Spectral Clustering, etc.) to algorithmically derive these clusters.

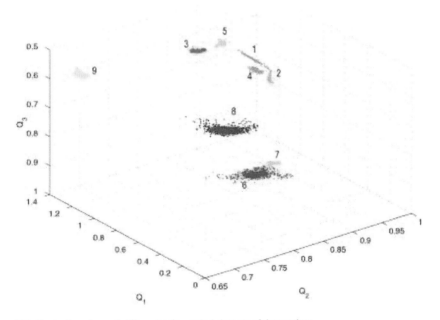

This illustration shows 9 different color-coded clusters of data points

But colleges get this segmentation for free, because each new student enrolls in a specific major: built-in segmentation. This segmentation is valuable because it allows Rio Salado to treat its different segments (majors, in this case) uniquely. For example, Rio Salado tested an interaction method in a Psychology class and it effectively raised retention and completion rates.

However, when they tried the same method in a math class, it had the opposite effect. With proper segmentation in place, Rio Salado is able to identify what methods work best for their different student groups, put action plans in place to retain their students, and surpass their competition.

Customer goals dictate how they interact with a business and what they want from it. For Colleges it's simple; students want to graduate, but for companies offering services it's more complicated. Your customers' goals will vary based on their industry, their customers, and their expectations. But more specifically, their goals will vary based on the segment they're in. Going back to our example, a math major may want to become a physicist, while biology majors might want to become veterinarians.

Knowing customers' goals allows companies to anticipate customer needs and move to satisfy them. For most business' understanding your customers goals forms the basis for your segmentation.

Clusters in your clusters

Once you know what segment a customer belongs to, you can tailor your interaction with them in order to provide the best possible experience. If you're lucky you can segment your customers easily.

The other side of Rio Salado's segmentation process is segmentation based on performance and predicted end result. Sub-segments within the major segments. Core to Rio Salado's success has been their three-tier risk assessment model that predicts the probability of a student passing the class given their current data. As early as 8 days in, students are put into High, Medium, and Low risk groups. Though their testing, They've established that: "The mean success rate was approximately 70% in the Low warning group, 54% in the Moderate warning group, and 34% in the High warning group.[2]" or

---

[2]Report on Rio Salado Community College Student Retention Program

in other words, the predictive model based on 8 days of data is statistically valid.

The way Rio Salado built these models is a lot like how Target built its "pregnancy projection" back in section 1.4. Both involved examining past data to find correlations and patterns in customer behaviors, and both were built to find those correlations before a certain point in time is reached.

The difference is in the implementation: Target started out looking for a specific behavior and directed its efforts at discovering the driver—it already knew the segment it needed (pregnant women). Customer retention as Rio Salado implemented it involves a few more steps: discovering the major segments, and then segmenting within those segments to discover who was and who was not following the desired trajectory.

Discovering the behaviors and traits responsible for driving behavior in the sub-groups is done using correlations.

Correlations

We talked briefly about correlations earlier—they're a remarkably powerful and fundamental part of data science, and in truth most of the insights we derive come from exposing correlations in some shape or form. At its core a correlation exposes a pattern in the data—hopefully one that we can act on.

Rio Salado identified a wide range of correlations in creating their student retention program, and these correlations have proven to be valuable because they suggest that doing 'A' could be partially responsible for passing the class, or that there is a common cause behind doing 'A' and passing your class. So if class participation strongly correlates with passing grades, then we can assume class participation partially causes students to have passing grades. Likewise, using WebMD is highly correlated with going to the doctor, so we can assume there could be a common cause to both: having an illness.

Now if you're clever, you might think, 'based on your previous conclusion, couldn't you say that using WebMD causes illness?" Yes, with limited information sometimes you can come up with ridiculous conclusions (although hypochondriacs going to WebMD might make themselves sick, but that's beside the point). This highlights an important part of data science: how interpretation is an integral part of understanding your data. That's something you will find over and over, data doesn't interpret itself.

Also, don't forget this key logical fallacy, which is extremely important to keep in mind at all times when looking at the output of data science:

Correlation does not imply causation.

Correlations don't prove anything on their own, it could be that class participation just happens to correlate with passing grades with no relationship existing between the two. The only way to verify the correlation is through testing. Do what you can to raise the participation of students and see if it impacts passing grades. In the real world, this is difficult to do because you simply can't isolate one variable very easily, but through testing we can establish high levels of confidence in our correlations.

This is also where the business experience aspect of data science comes into play: if you've been involved in the business operations you can easily use the "sniff test" to determine whether or not a specific correlation is worth paying attention to.

How to do this Really Well

Everything Rio Salado is able to do with segmentation and predictive modeling is based on their data. Like we discussed in the introduction, data is like oil, and the more of it you have the more you can earn from it. But one thing a lot of people miss is the potential to create more data/value from the data you already have.

An interesting thing about data is that it tends to "snowball"; the more you work with data the bigger it gets and the more you can do with it. This is one of those tricks you need to know, and it's also one of the tricks people normally forget about. This works to your advantage because if you can do it well, you'll have a significant advantage in your industry.

The general idea is that the more data you have, the more data you have access to. This may sound a little confusing, but in reality it's very simple. Say you have two sources of data, Data Source 1 and Data Source 2. They could be your sales data, a social network, sensor data, it doesn't really matter. If you can link the data in Data Source 1 to the data in Data Source 2, you can merge the two and come up with data that's theoretically twice as rich. We call this "Data Source Daisy Chaining".

But the real power lies in the fact that the combined data source of 1 and 2 may now have enough information to talk about your data with yet another data source, let's call it Data Source 3. Whereas neither Data Source 1 nor Data Source 2 alone may have enough data to link to Data Source 3, the combined data does. And that lets you start a snowball effect where the data source can become exponentially more rich and informative, which makes ALL of your algorithms work MUCH better.

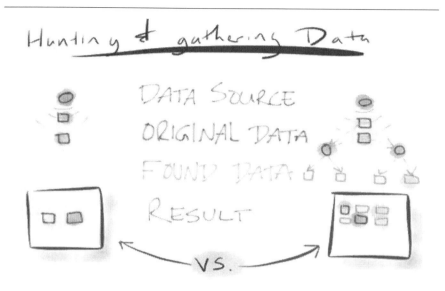

This illustrates a key point which, if you understand and use it, will transform your business. You need to integrate your data in order to see the types of results we talk about this in this book. Each data source may be an island, but your job is to build bridges.

CUSTOMER RETENTION BLUEPRINT

Customer retention is a key topic that deserves more attention than we can devote to it here. If you'd like to receive a FREE **Customer Retention Blueprint**, Click here to get it

http://bit.ly/12B5gPd

Part 2: Big Data

It's time to move on. So far the concepts and techniques we've covered aren't specific to Big Data—they can be used on normal-sized data just as easily. Now we're going to talk about the impact of Big Data and how it is influencing society.

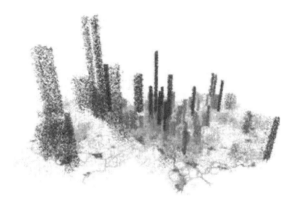

Section 2.1: What is Big Data?

What is Big Data? For many it's the buzzword they use to say they're using "bleeding edge" technology, and others use as a synonym for the challenges it brings. In truth, there is no uniformly accepted definition because people use the term to mean a wide variety of things to suit their purposes. It has been used to describe data tools, data sets, questions, problems and answers.

The way it is used most frequently by those in the industry - at least those who aren't pushing a particular agenda - also happens to be the most useful and simple understanding available: Big Data is data that is significantly large and growing larger fast. In other words Big Data is big data, and you know you have it when the size of your data is part of your problem.

Here's a dirty little secret of the industry: you might not actually have "big data". Big data typically comes from truly massive organizations such as governments, or from networks of sensors or other devices that produce data constantly (think of a thermometer that gives a reading every 0.1 second, for example). However, don't let that discourage you, because you can certainly get the value of these techniques and processes even if you only have a few hundred or thousand records. Inevitably your data will grow, and you'll need to be familiar with these topics.

A recent survey of data professionals asked them how large the largest data set they've ever analyzed was:

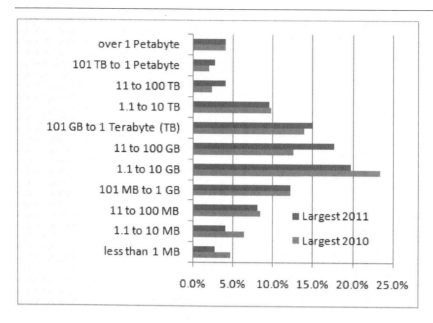

Keep in mind that these are the *largest* these respondents have *ever* analyzed, and you may realize that big data is sometimes not as big as it's made out to be.

Truly big data however presents a unique challenge because there's so much of it that traditional data management techniques can't keep up. When you're dealing with billions or trillions of records you can't back up your database on disk or tape, you can't transmit it over the network, and analyzing it becomes a unique challenge.

Beyond this definition, it is important to realize that data is also evolving, in some instances its structure is changing, but in all instances it is growing. This is part of the trouble with the term, if we put a size on it, then in five years it won't actually be big anymore because the data sets we'll be dealing with in five years will be so much larger than they are today.

Interview with a data legend: Dr. Andreas Weigend
Clearly the biggest societal shift in the past 20 years has been the consumerization of technology. As computers moved out of the IT staff and

into the mainstream the average person has first gotten online in the 1990's and then spent an increasing portion of their life online in the 2000's as social networks became popular. This migration to the Internet has spawned several different waves of social networks, notably AOL, then MySpace, and then Facebook and Twitter, followed by an undetermined next wave, and each has expanded the amount of data we create. We are at the point now where social data is the largest data category in both size and growth rate.

Dr. Andreas Weigend is an expert in social data, he teaches about it at Stanford University and directs their Social Data  Lab. He previously worked as Amazon's Chief Data Scientist and helped establish the customer-centric, data-focused culture the company is now known for. Having addressed the United Nations and advised influential companies, Dr. Weigend is shaping the data culture with his vision for how data can improve our lives. I recently had the pleasure of interviewing Dr. Weigend and talking about his views concerning the future of data.

JK: What is your dream for social data?

AW: I really do think it is transparency, something that used to be avoided by companies. Actually in the olden days, companies made money by creating information asymmetry; the used car salesmen is the classic example. Now companies make money by removing information asymmetry.

So the dream is to have a society where because of transparency more than big data, people will be more comfortable, there will be less corruption, and there will be fewer human rights violations. That would be my dream.

The problem is that every technology that can be used for good can also be used for evil, so the same thing that allowed the Arab Spring to happen, allowed the Pakistani terrorists to kill. By pinning down where the tweet happened and using Google to confirm that the guy looks that way, they can send someone in and boom, the guy is taken out.

JK: What would you like to see happen with social data in the next 5 years?

AW: it's less about data per se, then what it is used for; what will happen in the world based on social data. Starting with the obvious things, in the next five years we will create 10 times as much data as we create now, that's a fact, that our production rate doubles every half year. The second fact is that most of the data is social data. It's less what companies put out in their PR releases, more that machines create data and machines connected to people.

What I would like to see is data being used to create better products. How would I like to see companies benefit more from social data? By tightly integrating social data into their product design.

Let me give you an example. I am here in South Korea, where there is a large telephone company. In response to social data, they have changed their out of box experience when someone buys a phone. The old out of the box experience was awful. You didn't have your friends in there, you didn't have anywhere to go for help etc., whereas now the out of box experience of the phone I have here is absolutely amazing. You enter your Gmail and it does amazing things. Everything you would want loads automatically.

Social data will change the world of service. For more than a decade now, the trust people have in airlines and hotels is based more and more on social data. Not based on the hotel taking fancy pictures, but on people saying those cockroaches after three days finally receded. So that is useful data for products, second one is use social data for service.

JK: What obstacles do you see that could prevent these changes from happening?

AW: Product design and feedback, where institutional people just think that they know better, that designers know better, but those who just embrace the feedback loop will be the ones who benefit from social data.

For the second one, the services or information creation, it is the fear of the loss of control.

JK: How should we overcome those obstacles?

AW: Changing mindsets where people think it's about the datasets, but what it's really about is moving from dataset to toolset; then you move from toolset to skillset, that's what I teach my students at Stanford and Berkeley. But ultimately it's about the mindset, and it's about being willing to be open to put your insecurities about your product out in the world and let the world play with it in testing. The second one is putting out your insecurities that it might not be a perfect product and people will criticize it. One example is amazon reviews.

From the consumer side, my hope for the social data revolution in the next five years is that people will make their tradeoffs much more consciously and deliberately. So, I am sharing my geolocation and my hope is that we will see thought leaders, we'll see regulators actually push people towards thinking. So it's not "don't make me think", but it's 'yes! Please do make me think about the consequences of the social data I create and share'.

JK: What questions should we be asking about data?

AW: A good question... what it is the impact of social data on life? So we've been talking a lot about data, but the most important thing about it is life. How has the notion of life and work changed in the aftermath of social data? Consider smartphones for a moment, it's a good thing for when you're on a date because you don't have to talk with the other person anymore, you can just text people. So really, how has social data and technology impacted our lives?

Thanks to Dr. Weigend for taking the time for this interview. To learn more from Dr. Weigend go to www.weigend.com and subscribe to his YouTube channel Social Data Revolution.

The Big Data Challenge

When we talk about the Big Data Revolution, the promise it holds is right in front of us: far greater understanding of our world, removal of wasted or misused resources, and dramatically increased efficiency. In other words: better and more productive lives. To reach this dream, the Big Data Challenge must be addressed. There are three major challenges that need to be met to make this promised future a reality: get the data, manage it, and understand it. Our ability to capture and store data is severely outpacing our ability to analyze and understand it, and that is at the heart of the Big Data challenge.

Back in 2010, Eric Schmidt—then CEO of Google—stated that we now create as much data every 2 days as we did from the dawn of man through 2003. We are now producing far more data than we did in 2010. In fact, we create about 2.5 quintillion bytes of data daily and approximately 90% of all our world's data has been created in the past 2 years. Data, be it social or observed, is a driving force in human advancement when it can be recorded, measured, and analyzed; the current data explosion is the birth of a human revolution. The expansion in available information creates an awesome resource for the data revolution, but it's also a huge challenge.

At the March 2012 White House Big Data Initiative, the acting director of DARPA Ken Gabriel described the Big Data Challenge in more human terms. Gabriel compared Big Data to the Atlantic Ocean: "The Atlantic Ocean is 350m kilometers in volume -- 100 billion billion gallons." Gabriel stated, "If each gallon represents a byte, the Atlantic Ocean would only be able to store the data generated by the world in 2010." The ocean is huge and that's a lot of Data. Finding the useful information among all the noise? Well, Gabriel went on to say it's like searching the entire ocean for a 55 gallon drum barrel. This is the challenge: making sense of all that data and finding the value hidden in it.

So you can see the scope of this challenge—as of 2013 the amount of data is around 1200 exabytes and we have a problem when it comes to consuming that much data. The processes we're talking about are among the most advanced data science techniques available, and can do a lot to face this. However, the size and scope of data is growing fast and what we now consider Big Data will be paltry compared with what we'll be working with 10 years from now. So if we want to reach the data driven future we're looking forward to, then we need to focus on besting the big data challenge.

Section 2.3: Politics and Big Data

Although politicians might be a bit slow to adopt Big Data solutions for government problems and policy decisions, when it comes to running their campaigns they turn straight to Silicon Valley. The bigger the campaign, the more innovative they become, and the 2012 Obama campaign is the new gold standard.

One of the largest advances Obama's campaign developed was "Project Narwhal", a data warehousing project that unified information and gave Obamas campaign the ability to target people in ways that were previously impossible.

"Key to the campaign's success was a technology platform that allowed us to engage with constituents and make data-driven decisions in real time," claims Michael Slaby, Obama's chief information and innovation officer.

Although it sounds more like a part of the Dharma Initiative than an actual organization, "Project Narwhal" changed the way politics works.

Narwhal – Mythical Unicorn of the sea

Narwhal's goal was quite simple: build a unified political profile of each individual voter. Large-scale campaigns gather data about the electorate in many different ways for different purposes, and this leads to a scattered understanding of voters. Narwal took all of the data, from tweets to donations and everything in between, and created unified individual profiles for each voter.

Back in 2008, data wasn't managed collectively, "Every unit within the campaign had their little fiefdom and a chief. People were very proprietary about their data," an Obama 2008 staffer said. "They started as separate systems because that's the way it works. No one ever thought System B would get useful data for System A—and we weren't planning for the long run from the beginning."

But 2012 was different: the campaign realized that fusing the data would provide a more comprehensive picture of the electorate. Full data integration in real time allowed the campaign to target voters in ways previously only imagined. One of the more visible uses was to tailor messages to individual recipients. Few people agree 100% with Obama's entire platform, but with Narwhal working in the background, every message you saw from the campaign featured just the policies you loved. Where you disagreed, you never knew.

The result: A database containing unique profiles on an estimated 16 million voters, volunteers, and donors, a database that helped Obama raise over $181 million through email marketing in one month alone.

If you're familiar with traditional survey processes, you can already see why this is revolutionary. A large survey, for political purposes, is about 500 responses. Believe it or not, these are the samples that our politicians are using to base their campaigns on. Moving into technology like that of Project Narwhal, however, you're suddenly talking about a database orders of magnitude larger. Aside from being more representative of the entire population, the data will become much, much richer at that size, exposing patterns and correlations that were hidden with smaller data sets.

> One thing to keep in mind as you continue exploring big data is that when you deal with large numbers you begin talking about probabilities. If Narwhal predicts my feelings about gun control and they're wrong, it may not have the desired effect on me. But over thousands of people it will be mostly right, and the benefit of those people outweighs the cost of losing me as an individual.

Project Narwhal's fundraising magic comes from two primary functionalities: its unique understanding of each recipient, and its ability to split test. Because it analyzes Twitter and any other interactions you had with the campaign, it was able to build a very full profile of you simply based on how similar you are to other people that you're similar to. This resulted in Narwhal understanding many of your beliefs and convictions, enabling it to send you targeted emails about them.

The project also helped logistically; last time around when volunteers canvassed neighborhoods they simply went door to door. But in 2012, armed with detailed maps about neighborhood residents and optimized talking points, canvassers skipped the hardcore supporters on either side of the political spectrum (who were already decided anyway) and got right to the elusive undecided voting blocks.

Big Data Warehousing

We talked briefly about data warehousing earlier, now it's time to talk about how data warehousing needs to respond to the challenge of big data.

Again, data warehousing is the process of taking data from multiple sources, cleaning it up and making it uniform, and then placing it into a common storage area (the data warehouse). From there, the data warehouse can be used by business intelligence and analytics tools to look at all of the data from the different data sources as a whole—instead of as segregated data sources.

Data warehousing allows an apples to apples comparison instead of apples to oranges.

Data warehousing becomes a bit more complex when we're talking about huge amounts of data; typically the tools and hardware you'll use is specialized to the task.

The key word here is **scalability.** This is a word you'll hear often in computer and data science, and it simply means that ability for the tool set you're using to accommodate the load you're throwing at it. Big Data is special because it requires a different toolset to scale.

As a brief aside, you'll often hear about two different types of scalability, and it's handy to remember which is the limiting factor when you're looking at big data tools:

- **Horizontal** scalability is the ability to scale simply by adding more servers, typically cheap commodity servers. This is the Google approach to big data, and it's currently by far the most desirable way to scale. Although this will be argued by vendors who offer tools that use...
- **Vertical scaling**, which is the ability to scale by adding more hardware to existing servers. The reason this isn't as desirable is because A) you have to take the servers offline to add capacity and B) it takes more time to upgrade a server than to spin up a new one, and it's more brittle—you can't very effectively "un-upgrade" a server if you need to.

Now let's take a look at the tools in the Big Data toolset.

Section 2.4: The Big data toolset

There are two main categories of big data tools that you'll see referenced: databases and data crunchers. No these are not exact terms, but the tools you run into will most often fall into one of these categories.

DataBases: Relational Vs. noSQl

There are two main types of database: relational and NoSQL. Relational databases have been in use forever, and NoSQL databases are relatively newer and more in vogue at the moment.

Relational databases are so called because they keep track of the relationships between objects. For example, a relational database will know which sales belong to a particular customer because those relationships are encoded within the database itself. The most popular relational databases include:

- Oracle
- MySQL
- Microsoft SQL Server

(But there are many, many more.)

NoSQL databases do not maintain these relationships, it's up to the applications that use them to track these things. NoSQL databases got their name because the first generation of them didn't support a specific data query language called SQL which was developed to talk to relational databases (hence "no SQL"). Today many NoSQL databases actually *do* support queries via SQL, and so the term has been repurposed to mean "Not Only SQL".

Another notable characteristic of NoSQL databases, and the reason they're popular, is because of the way they store data on the server's disk. Instead of storing data according to their relationships they store data in very large rows called columns within the files on the disk. This is arguably more scalable and support horizontal scalability much better. In fact if you hear the term "columnar database" this is probably what's being referred to.

There are several popular NoSQL databases available today, including:

- Apache Cassandra
- HBase
- MongoDB

Most of these projects, if they're open source (which the majority in use today are), were developed by large consumer Internet companies such as Twitter and Facebook to handle the amount of data they were generating. Thankfully they've open sourced these projects and we're free to use them today.

Data crunchers

This is, in my opinion, the most interesting part of Big Data—the tools that have been developed to cope with intense analysis of huge amounts of data. For example, Excel is a fantastic tool for analyzing data, but it cannot and will not be able to process the amounts of data that we're talking about here.

The thing that most of these tools have in common is that they were developed to chop up huge quantities of data into smaller bite-sized chunks so that the processing load can be spread across many servers (again, this is called horizontal scalability).

Most of the tools we'll be talking about can be made to work with just about any database, so you aren't restricted to specific NoSQL databases to use them.

Map-Reduce

Map reduce is quite famous in the Big Data community. It is not a product or a specific piece of software, but rather a technology developed by Google to deal with large amounts of data by chopping it up, and then recombining it at the end. Many of the tools we'll cover adopt this principle in some way inside the tool itself.

We'll spend a little time explaining how this works because this idea of spreading load around many servers is a cornerstone concept for dealing with massive amounts of data.

The basic idea is that data that needs to be processed enters the system, and is chopped into bite-size chunks. The piece of software that does that chopping is called a "mapper". (These terms aren't very intuitive, don't worry about it.) The chunks are then sent to another piece of software that does the required processing on them, and then they're sent to yet another piece of software called "reducers" which combine the end result back together for output.

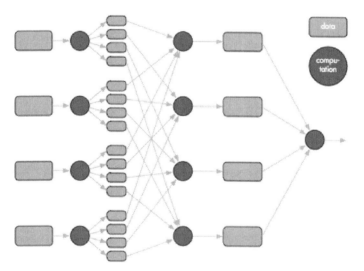

All of these pieces of software—the mapper, processor, and reducer—typically run on many servers at once. This way, the load of processing the mapped (chopped up) data can be spread across all available servers, and more servers can be added in real-time if you need a result faster.

It's not terribly important that you're familiar with how this all works. What is important is that you understand what the end result is—you're able to take a large chunk of data that no single server could handle on its own and distribute that processing load across a large number of servers. The tools we'll talk about next implement this paradigm.

Hadoop

Hadoop is an open-source project, overseen by the Apache Foundation that provides a structured environment to run  Map-Reduce jobs in. It is by far the most well-known and popular Map-Reduce implementation.

One of the knocks on Hadoop is that it's meant for batch processing—that is, data is grouped into batches to be processed, which means there's a delay between the input and output. It's not very well suited to real-time analysis, if that's what you need.

Hadoop has a great ecosystem of partners and projects built to support it. And if you're a large company who wants 24x7 support for your big data infrastructure, it's probably where you want to focus.

If you want to be more bleeding edge though, there are a few other options that provide slightly different or better functionality.

For example, one of the up and coming projects gaining a lot of momentum lately is called Storm, developed by a Twitter employee. It uses the same Map-Reduce paradigm but it operates on individual bits of data in real-time, rather than processing data in batches. As you can imagine, this is extremely beneficial when you need results immediately.

Section 2.5: Big data and healthcare

What would it be like to have a doctor who's always up on the latest research and has learned about treatments from over 1.5 million previous cases? It would look a lot like Watson, IBM's *Jeopardy!* playing supercomputer that's getting ready to roll out with an all new look and a Memorial Sloan Kettering Cancer Center education in oncology.

"It will be like having a Memorial Sloan Kettering trained colleague for any doctor on earth," claims Dr. Mark Kris, an MSKCC oncologist. "The goal here is to be part of the relationship between doctor and patient."

Unlike IBM's previous entrant in the man vs. machine battle, the chess playing computer Deep Blue, Watson is set to go commercial and earn IBM a healthy profit. Taking the data query and natural language processing tools developed while learning *Jeopardy!*, Wilson is getting a top ranked medical education and aiming to be the all-knowing decision support system that will transform the medical field.

"The power of the technology is that it has the ability to take the information about a specific patient and match it to a huge knowledge base and history of treatment of similar patients." stated Dr. Kris, "This process can help medical professionals gain important insights so that they can make more informed decisions, evidence based decisions, about what treatment to follow. Watson's ability to mine massive quantities of data means that it can also keep up – at record speeds – with the latest medical breakthroughs reported in scientific journals and meetings."

This is a terrific application for Watson. Medical knowledge is growing faster than anyone can keep up with, and no adequate technology exists to help doctors maintain awareness about new discoveries in their fields. The medical field currently produces so much new research that a doctor would have to spend 160 hours a week reading in order to stay informed. These reports can mean the difference between life and death, but without proper tools doctors simply don't know about them. Enter Watson medical assistant, IBM has retooled him to use the data query tools and natural language interpretation skills he perfected on *Jeopardy!* to be a new type of tool to help doctors solve this problem. Watson will in essence be an artificial brain interpreting all the data available, and giving doctors recommendations based on current research.

What does this mean for healthcare?
Watson powered healthcare could be a truly transformative technology and the biggest thing to ever come from IBM; the potential is truly staggering. This will play out in two ways, both are already being tested: patient care and financing.

At least six instances of Watson are currently deployed at partnering healthcare facilities, and doctors are using Watson to help patients suffering from lung, breast, and prostate cancer. Using its superior knowledge of research and patient records, Watson is already helping doctors determine the best course of action for each individual patient.

Watson helps in every phase of healthcare, from diagnosing to treating, and functions much like a conventional doctor. By examining the patient's electronic medical record (EMR), Watson builds a profile of the patient that it cross references with research, and suggests questions that will help build a deeper understanding of the patient's condition. Based on answers to questions and the EMR, Watson suggests possible tests that could help diagnose the patient. Throughout the whole process, Watson suggests treatment options and medical trials for the patient, and these suggestions have varying levels of confidence depending on available information. Low confidence likely means that more tests or questions should be used before treatment is administered.

So far, Watson is performing wonderfully and drastically improving performance. Studies have shown that while doctors are correct in their cancer diagnosis about 50% of the time, Watson is right 90% of the time.

IBM is also partnering with Wellpoint to tackle the financial side of healthcare. Using the same diagnostic method used for patient care, Watson is helping the insurance company determine whether or not a particular treatment is the best option for the patient financially. The implications of this role may be even more disruptive to healthcare than the improvement to patient care.

The skyrocketing cost of healthcare in the United States is severely damaging citizens, both economically and physically. Health insurance is expensive and only going up, while quality is dipping below that of other countries. It is absolutely possible that Watson could make a difference in this growing problem.

IBM estimates that $2.3 trillion of healthcare expenses are wasted, and believes Watson will drastically reduce that number. By finding the best possible treatment plan for people, both economically and physically, Watson could reduce the per-patient cost for insurance companies as well as individuals. This could effectually lower healthcare costs for everyone, and make it possible for hospitals to better use their resources.

How it works

To cook up this magic, IBM mixes many of the techniques we've covered earlier in the book coupled with some big data sauce. Watson is great because it's a perfect and very visible demonstration of data science and big data, so it makes a really interesting case study for us.

Let's break down how Watson arrives at its incredibly accurate diagnoses. (Which is going to be similar to the way it answers questions on Jeopardy.) If we wanted to duplicate Watson's functionality, how could we do it?

I actually happen to have a burning interest in self-healthcare using Quantified Self (self-recorded) data. I want it for myself. I won't go into it much here because it's kind of a tangent with some passion behind it. But at a 500-ft level it's all about using the increasing number of sensors we carry around with us at all times (pedometer, heart rate monitors, phones, smart watches, now Google glass) to effortlessly record all sorts of data about an individual. What I'm interested in is taking that data and making Watson-like predictions using that data.

So I've spent a lot of time thinking about these problems and have a pretty good idea of what's involved in technology like Watson.

The end goal of course, is to predict the effectiveness of a treatment for a specific patient. To know that we need to be able to rank all available treatments (including doing nothing) by their predicted effectiveness, and pick the best one off the top.

1. We will find this out by breaking down all of the patients in our system by their most important characteristics—that is, the characteristics that explain the most information. This is done using an algorithm such as Principle Component Analysis,

2. Next we need to cluster the customers using the primary characteristics revealed in the first step. It is **the exact same idea** we talked about in Section 1.6 as Amazon clusters its customers as they browse the site to determine recommended items.

3. Once the clusters have been discovered, the historical data about the treatment in question—but only for the group that the patient is actually in—is loaded into a trainer and used to build a model of that cluster. The model contains the rules for predicting how well a particular treatment will work on any member of a specific cluster of patients. The model will provide the probability of a specific outcome for a treatment for the patient.

4. Repeat this process for all treatments, and select the treatment the highest probability of a good outcome.

All of the above is possible using small data—there's nothing exceptionally challenging about these things in terms of size.

The big data part of this comes into play when we consider the data that IBM is bringing into the Watson system, which is unstructured text data in the form of medical studies. We'll cover unstructured data next.

What a fascinating future we're looking forward to. We spend a lot of time developing these specific ideas and if you're interested in this as well you should download our free Healthcare Blueprint.

HEALTH CARE ANALYTICS
BLUEPRINT

We're so excited about the potential of big data to completely revolutionize healthcare that we're developing a free **Healthcare Analytics Blueprint**, Click here to get it

http://bit.ly/19hfSEl

Section 2.6: Making Sense of Unstructured Data

It's hard to overstate how advanced the 2012 Obama Campaign was. In fact it was so advanced that Democrats are fighting to get access to the technology even now, and Republicans are scrambling to catch up.

Project Narwhal was just one of the major projects of the Obama Campaign. The other undertaking was called Project Dreamcatcher and was designed to learn about your passions.

Hopes and dreams, and fears and frustrations, these are the marketer's goldmines. They are the difference between telling you why you should buy something and making you feel that you need to buy it. You see it when you look at the difference between a product sold as a checklist of features versus one sold on emotion and sex. This was Project Dreamcatcher's goal.

Starting with the 2008 election the Obama campaign has gathered masses of unstructured data. From tweets about the president and his opponents to stories supporters post on his website, this data represents a treasure trove of usable knowledge.

The campaign has been particularly closed mouthed about Project Dreamcatcher, stating that, "We have no plans to read out our data/analytics/voter contact strategy. That just telegraphs to the other guys what we're up to." But as best as we can deduce Dreamcatcher relies on large scale text analysis to glean voters hopes and fears, and understand their positions on various political policies.

The people involved with the project said it analyzed text in an effort to unlock whole areas of personal information that has yet to be collected or put to use. The dream is to enable better decision making on which voters to target and how to do it.

"It's not about us trying to leverage the information we have to better predict what people are doing. It's about us being better listeners," a campaign official said. "When a million people are talking to you at once it's hard to listen to everything, and we need text analytics and other tools to make sense of what everyone is saying in a structured way."

One dream that big data makes plausible is the creation of a perfectly tailored world. A world where what you want to see and what you want to learn more about is always in front of you; the things you don't see are only those things you don't care about. Dreamcatcher strived to create this type of tailored world for Obama, showing voters just what they wanted to see.

> We have to be careful when talking about this type of technology. There are many people who feel that this sort of information-tailoring is a very bad thing because it results in a myopic view of the world. But our job here is not to take one side or the other, it's to talk about the technology.

How it Works

Data either has structure or it doesn't. I can either say:

"I had a cheeseburger at 2:15"

Or I can send you a row of data that says the same thing:

Customer	Product	Time
Jason	Cheeseburger	2:15

The sentence is unstructured, the record is structured. They both contain the same information, in different ways. And computers have been working with both of them forever.

The difference here is that **turning unstructured data into structured data** requires some of the technology that we've talked about earlier—training models, probabilities, and so forth. It's not an exact science, because language itself isn't very exact sometimes. This is what happens when you talk to Siri on your iPhone.

You and I create masses of data every day. Every tweet, every status update, every blog you post, every email you send and image you share creates data, and for the most part it's unstructured data.

Around 95% of the data we create in a day is unstructured, and just like structured data, unstructured holds great value if only we can access it.

Structured data is data that has been coded, classified, and organized in such a way that it can be analyzed using Data Science practices. Think spreadsheets when you think structured data, it really is data built for computers.

Unstructured data in contrast, is stuff that is built for you and I to consume— blog posts, tweets, status updates, emails, audio and video files. It's all data, but it is harder for computers to understand. Until recently, the only thing we could do with this type of information was enjoy it, or not, depending on its quality. This type of information isn't built for computers to analyze, it is built for people.

What Project Dreamcatcher does is build structure into unstructured data so that it can be classified and analyzed. In particular, the project explored massive amounts of text in order to analyze the sentiment of the writers about various topics. Watson does the same thing, but it reads medical journals and clinical trial results.

Natural language processing

Natural Language Processing (NLP) has been around for a long time. It's typically not considered part of the core data science toolkit because it has very specific use cases. But should the need arise, you'll want to employ a tool built specifically for that purpose.

The models involved in language analysis tend to get very complex, and they take a long time to perfect on your own. For example, one of the more popular uses of natural language analysis tools is to tag a single sentence with the parts of speech of each of the words.

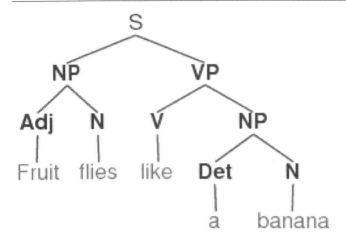

The letters are codes for various parts of speech—NP for Noun Phrase, N for Noun for example. Software can take this information and incorporate it into its own models for determining topics being talked about, frequency, and so on.

In order to accomplish this, large models are built by running over huge selections of text—all of the Supreme Court rulings for the last 100 years, or the entire last 25 years of the Wall Street Journal.

Fortunately there are several open source projects that you can tap into. These projects all vary in their implementations, and it's not clear right now whether any of the approaches are better than the other.

- Apache OpenNLP is built in Java, has been around for a while, and is well-supported.
- NLTK is smaller and written in Python but has some interesting features.
- Stanford has a highly-regarded open source natural language toolkit (although you must purchase a commercial license to use it commercially).
- LingPipe is the most well-known commercial offering, and it does speed the time to implement things such as sentiment analysis.

But at the end of the day, keep in mind that that this entire exercise is done to produce structured data from unstructured. For example, sentiment analysis runs a chunk of text through a trained model and produces a score (from -5.0 to +5.0, for example), representing that aspect of the text. The result is structured data which has been derived from the unstructured data.

Section 2.7: Data Disrupting Government

Shortly before being appointed to the Supreme Court in 1906, Louis Brandeis famously made a quote about corruption and secrecy:

"Publicity is justly commended as a remedy for social and industrial diseases. Sunlight is said to be the best of disinfectants; electric light the most efficient policeman. And publicity has already played an important part in the struggle against the Money Trust."

It's easy to become disillusioned with government. Incompetence, corruption and waste are so baked into our current system that it can feel pointless to even try to make a difference. And unfortunately for us today the so-called "fourth estate", the Press, is doing a poor job of casting sunlight on things that should not be hidden.

Fortunately, government is an area where data is readily available, and people are pushing hard for more open data in government. As a result, the data is just sitting around waiting to be exposed.

Governments have been collecting data for internal use for centuries. The British Royal Statistical Society, of which Charles Babbage was a prominent member, has been collecting interesting data for a long, long time:

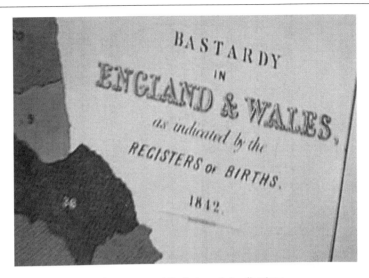

Early government Big Data and visualizations

But only recently have the technical tools been available to allow governments to expose this data using things like public API's, data exports, and so on.

The Big Data Revolution is changing our world. And it's going to change government quite a bit before all is said and done. Data is doing the job the Press was supposed to do by extracting hidden insights about the government, and in some ways, it is establishing a Fifth Estate: the Data Science Estate.

A wealth of government data is available to us today on .gov sites and private sites across the web. If we analyzed this data properly, we could build a rich understanding of how our government works and how it could be improved. But as the big data challenge dictates, the chokepoint is consumption.

Back in 2004, data scientists from Columbia conducted a thorough exploration of roll call voting data (a small amount of data by today's standards) which is publicly available through the Library of Congress online. Using the tools available at the time, they did cluster analysis, pattern recognition, 3D metric mapping, and more to provide a rather deep look into the workings of the US senate. Their primary findings explored the differing clusters within congress, and even showed just how influential certain politicians were. It's worth checking out (http://bit.ly/Wr5mFK).

If they built so much with so little what can today's data scientists do?

Several organizations are trying to find out. They're gathering massive amounts of data and helping us understand what that data means. By creating tools allowing you to track expenditures, watch your representatives, check voting records, and examine campaign contributions, sites such as govtrack.us and influenceexplorer.com are peeling back the curtain to reveal the hidden side of politics.

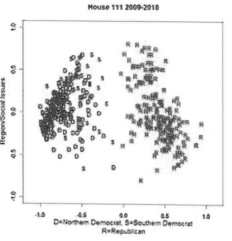

Govtrack lets you see how politicians are voting and where they fit on the political spectrum, and with Influence Explorer you can see where they got their money from. Both sites use large amounts of data to display valuable information about politics, but they fall short because they rely on users to take that information and make it usable.

The dream of Big Data and Government is for all these data sources to be unified and explored, which could truly open our eyes. We could quantify the effect money has on politicians, heck you could give each politician a rating based on what degree they favor their backers over their constituents. This could also help politicians by helping them see how much they are being affected. You have probably heard the adage, "if you can measure it, you can manage it" well big data can measure it.

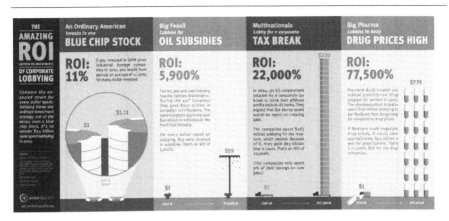

Data is huge, and if used well it has the potential to hold the government accountable in amazing ways. This type of reporting and analysis is in its infancy and has been largely unused, but we see the potential, the promised land of government transparency, transparency born from Big Data and Analytics.

Part 3: Tools of the Trade

Section 3.1: Current Business Intelligence and Data Discovery tools.

We're at a curious place now, a shift from old to new. The tools that dominated the industry for decades are starting to show their age and a new wave of tools is looking to fix the problem.

And there's a specific problem that people have with current tools which is going to be solved very shortly.

Shortly after I sold my BI software company to Cisco in 2007, I remember walking into a Fortune 100 company that wanted more insight into the interactions they had with their customers. It was the day after we finished installing our sweet new Web 2.0 business intelligence application (it was the first completely Web-based tool, as a matter of fact). The director who oversaw customer contacts wanted to see what it could do. (This was in the Web 2.0 heyday, where "Web 2.0" was the magic pill that would fix all of your business problems and your back problems at the same time.)

"So, what can it tell me?" he asked me.

"What do you want to know?" was my quite logical reply.

He said "I'm not sure. Can you just show me something interesting?"

And that, ladies and gentlemen, is the problem with Business Intelligence in a nutshell.

That is why Business Intelligence is going to die.

I'm fortunate to have sold that company to Cisco back in 2007, and I still have a certain fondness for it, but that product was a bastion of old-school Business Intelligence. It was very, very good at giving you answers to your questions. But that type of product is going to die.

"But," you ask, "isn't data hotter than hot!?" 4 out of the past 5 years CIOs surveyed by Gartner Research labeled data strategies as the most important area for development, and news about data mining and analytics is finding its way into mainstream media.

You know about Data Science and its potential, how it creates greater understanding of our world, reveals hidden potential, reduces waste, and dramatically increases efficiency. The level of information available is growing like never before, and hiding in all that data are the insights, ideas, opportunities, and explanations needed to reach that promised potential; it's just waiting to be discovered—and there's the problem.

Traditional BI cannot keep up with the amount of data and it can't keep up with the transforming landscape of the data industry, and most importantly:

It can only answer questions that you already know you should be asking.

The Crushing Weight of Big Data.

Traditional business intelligence vendors struggle with Big Data. Their tools were built before the cloud was a buzzword and are meant to live in traditional data centers where it's much more desirable to scale up— vertically, by adding hardware to existing servers—than out. These tools were built to analyze the amount of data than can fit on a server, or if you're really fancy, a cluster of servers.

These tools weren't built in a distributed mindset (for example, by using Map-Reduce ideas). They aren't designed to sift through massive data warehouses, and they can't identify what is meaningful or what should be ignored. They simply present reports and dashboards on top of your data, in response to questions you tell it you need to know the answers to. It turns the answers into a pretty collection of charts, graphs, and grids that you can read on a daily, weekly, or monthly basis.

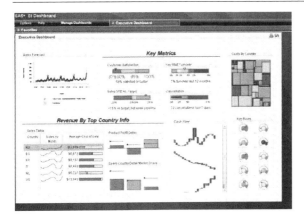

Pretty, but does it matter?

Millions went into the development of some of these programs, but they were designed for days gone by. Now companies are attempting to update for Big Data by duct-taping on tools like Hadoop. But the fact remains that they are built for a paradigm where you have to know the question before you can get an answer.

But what if you **don't** know the questions you should be asking? Well that's a problem. Because, quite frankly, that is where all of the interesting stuff is.

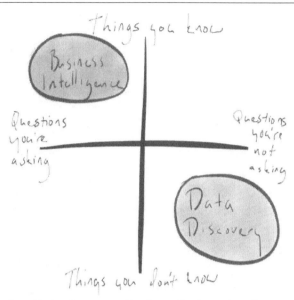

And let's be clear that when we talk about Business Intelligence we're really talking about a class of product, not the intelligence that comes from data, directed towards business. Two very different things. There's a clear class of software that emerged in the 1990's and 2000's that is labeled "business intelligence", and that's what we're talking about. This includes things such as dashboards, emailed reports, OLAP cubes to an extent, and so on. "Business intelligence" in the sense of the intelligence derived from data that's applicable to your business is clearly not dying, that's the whole point.

And it's important to note that business intelligence applications still do have a place: they're excellent at disseminating information. Once you've found something interesting, business intelligence tools are perfect vehicles for delivering that information to a wider audience and hopefully collaborating on it with others.

We're going to focus primarily on data discovery for a while because that's where we believe the most opportunity lies. But if you'd like to learn more about business intelligence—the process of deploying these tools and getting value from them—you should check out our earlier book on this exact topic.

Introduction to Business Intelligence

A practical guide to Data Mining and Business Analytics

To learn more about business intelligence as a practice and how it's implemented, you might want to think about checking out our earlier book focused entirely on this topic. It's a foundational text for understanding the business intelligence world. It covers the entire process of BI from data collection and storage through the different means of data analytics.

You can find it on Amazon

The Transforming Landscape

People have recently become aware of the world-changing power of data to make and remake industries. And, truth be told, that movement is still in its infancy, we're just now starting to understand the ramifications in society, business, and culture. The volume of data quickly shows BI for what it is: outdated. BI simply cannot put Big Data to work for its customers.

People see the potential and they want to use the tools to unlock it, but a short look at any of the current BI tools shows just how difficult that is for a non-data scientist. BI tools are primarily designed for IT and CIOs, if you want to use it you need to be trained. But as society at large moves towards a data-driven approach to, well, everything, a much larger audience for data tools is emerging: a whole new type of customer, non-technical, and a much larger market that traditional BI tools just can't reach.

Beyond this, what end-users want from BI has changed. Traditional BI is fantastic at building reports and monitoring key performance indicators, but it uses dashboards, grids, and tables primarily to show the data. This type of reporting is fantastic if you already know all of the questions you should be asking, but most people without a data scientist or five to lean on don't know this.

Fortunately, there are new tools becoming available which fill this gap. Forward-thinking companies and startups are creating solutions which make it easy to explore data and find answers. We classify these types of tools as "Data Discovery" tools—they make it easy (or at least, easier) to find the interesting facts within the mountains of available data.

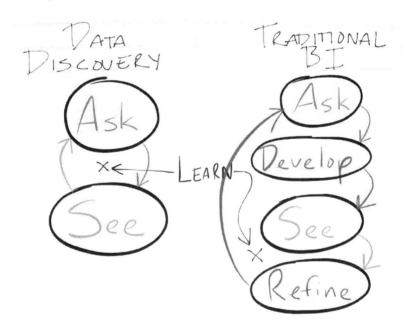

In addition to only providing answers and no questions, BI apps have another knock on them—if you want to see something new there's a lag time. Typically there's some level of setup that needs to be done in order to answer a new question. If you look at a report and see something interesting, you'll have to get in touch with the technical person responsible for running the product to have a new report made to answer that question. If that prompts another question you need to go through this cycle again.

Data discovery tools, on the other hand, are built to empower the end-user to investigate on his own in real-time (or close to it). If you see something interesting you can drill into it immediately and continue to iterate in that way.

The analytics market is bifurcating—splitting into two segments: the old "business intelligence" market and the new "data discovery" market. Gartner Research speaks to this in their latest Business Intelligence Magic Quadrant report:

"Data discovery alternatives to enterprise BI platforms offer highly interactive and graphical user interfaces built on in-memory architectures to address business users' unmet ease-of-use and rapid deployment needs. What began as a market buying trend in 2010 has only continued to expand. Sales results for vendors in this sector have been stellar and well above the market average. The two branches of BI can be defined as follows:

- Enterprise BI platforms:
    - Key buyers: IT.
    - Main sellers: megavendors, large independents.
    - Approach: top-down, IT-modeled (semantic layers), query existing repositories.
    - User interface: report/KPI dashboard/grid.
    - Use case: monitoring, reporting.
    - Deployment: consultants.
- Data discovery platforms:

- o Key buyers: business.
- o Main sellers: small, fast-growing independents.
- o Approach: bottom-up, business-user-mapped (mashup), move data into dedicated repository.
- o User interface: visualization.
- o Use case: analysis.
- o Deployment: users.

The chasm between these segments continues to deepen because business users find the benefits of using data discovery tools so compelling."

We agree completely with Gartner, and we believe that this trend will only accelerate over the medium-to-long-term. Data discovery capabilities will become increasingly important as the amount of data continues to increase and the traditional business intelligence fails to keep up.

Back in 2007 this didn't help me much, I didn't have a good answer for the director. Today it's a slightly different story: the tools are improving, becoming smarter. There are tools becoming available that can help mine for the nuggets of gold in the sea of data. That's called Data Discovery.

With Data Discovery, the technology is built around enabling you to mine data for yourself, or letting you use your imagination and intuition to find meaningful information about your data. This process usually consists of asking questions of the data in some way, seeing results visually, and refining the questions. Contrast this with the traditional approach which is for information consumers to ask questions, which causes reports to be developed, which are then fed to the consumer, which may generate more questions, which will generate more reports.

Data Discovery is gaining so much momentum because it allows you to move much faster. The answer to a question arrives immediately and can be thrown away in favor of a better question, and this can be repeated indefinitely, there is no lead time. Traditional business intelligence requires development time, which causes the questions to be "stickier"—if the question is wrong you're often hesitant to throw away the original work and start over, so the report is tweaked and refined until some semblance of an answer can be found, and at that point a new question can be asked and the process starts over again. Data discovery allows you to throw away work if it proves to be meaningless or unhelpful, it makes insight both disposable and a renewable resource.

This process is often referred to as "exploratory analytics" or "investigative analytics" due to its iterative nature and the way you "follow your nose" through your data. It's easily the most radical shift that business intelligence has seen in the past 20 years. Data discovery embodies using technology to augment human capabilities, which is very often proven to be more effective than humans alone, or technology alone.

Because of this symbiotic workflow—you might even say necessitated by it—data discovery tools are often much easier to use than traditional business intelligence tools. They're intended to be used by the end users of the information, not by an IT department or developer, and so much of the complexity has been abstracted away and made invisible. It's much more complex to develop these tools, but much, much easier to use them.

For example in the hands of an advanced user, Excel could be considered a very good data discovery tool—it does in fact allow easy navigation of data and quick, interactive question asking. In fact Microsoft often touts it as a data discovery tool. However, it fails the smell test in that it requires extensive training in Excel to be able to proficiently use it in a "real" data discovery method, and most business users don't have that much time to invest.

Data discovery tools often tend to be more visual and interactive than traditional reporting is. They employ radical new data visualization methods—charts, graphs, infographics, and so on—to display the results and prompt the user to new insights and ideas. In fact, data discovery has often been referred to as "visual data mining".

The most exciting aspect of data discovery in my opinion is the trend towards simplicity and ease of use, which will open up the wonders of analytics to a much wider audience over time. So let's take a moment to look at some of the top competitors in this market.

HEADS UP!

As the world continues to move into the cloud and away from in-house data centers, there's one aspect you should be on the lookout for: on premise-based software enterprise powerhouses are going to start fighting to maintain revenue streams. I'm sure they'd love to lock in those revenue streams in a way that's mutually beneficial - perhaps by renewing long-term contracts for steep discount - there's a more insidious way for them to accomplish this: data lock-in.

Software accumulates data, that's simply what it does. And that data is highly valuable because it holds insights about you and your business; it is the foundation of analytics. So one of the risks of putting data into a platform is that you won't be able to get it out. Switching software comes with a high price tag for transferring data, and your ability to get your data in and out of applications is in the hands of your vendors.

Because the switching cost is completely at the mercy of your current software, it's relatively easy for vendors to quietly raise that cost, especially if they're afraid of eroding revenues. Apple is notorious for doing this, by making it impossible to sync iTunes with non-iPhones, for example.

One of the unfortunate side effects of this behavior is that it's very possible to cripple the software as a side-effect of increasing switching costs. If a vendor makes it harder to get data out of a system it also makes it harder for third parties to use that data for other useful purposes:

> Business intelligence and analytics tools might not be able to get to the data
> Specialized backup tools often require direct access to data

Other applications often interact with enterprise system by looking at and possibly even modifying the data directly

Enterprise software vendors realize this, so they're hesitant to take this access away. However, it's easy to claim doing it in the name of security hardening or something. Given a good reason and a sufficient amount of desperation, it's a tempting policy to a CEO watching his profits steadily decline.

TAKEAWAYS

Understand why enterprise software vendors may be pushing for long-term contracts

Look out for updates from vendors that makes your software more closed

Data Discovery Tools

The relatively new data discovery field is growing at a surprising rate, both in the number of companies competing and the industries market share of the larger data analytics industry; According to Gartner's 2011 Data Discovery Tools report "Data discovery will be a $1 billion market in its own right as soon as 2013". However, It is a relatively small market compared to older technologies such as business intelligence (the number of business intelligence tools far outpaces the number of data discovery tools).

Data discovery tools generally work alongside their users to uncover hidden insights in data in an interactive and visual way. Because of this, you could almost consider data discovery tools to be data intelligence tools. Data discovery tools tend to be more visual and interactive than traditional reporting. They employ radical new data visualization methods—charts, graphs, infographics, and so on—to display the results and prompt the user to new insights and ideas. In fact, data discovery has often been referred to as "visual data mining".

If you're interested in data discovery tools we've put together an easy-to-read report which you'll find useful that compares the market leaders in a number of useful ways.

http://bit.ly/VZX19F

Section 3.3: industry-specific tools

The startup culture challenges established trends and innovates in truly fascinating ways. Everybody, from your small town coffee shop to roadside tamale stands produce data. The challenge is gathering and using it, and startups keep finding new ways to do just that.

We really enjoy hearing about novel ways people are using data, it tends to add perspective and make the techniques we've been talking about more concrete.

One recent novel use of data is in dairy farming. Farmeron, a software-as-a-service (SaaS) startup, is using the cloud to bring farming into the 21st century through product analytics.

Most companies have significant data about their products; procedural data, operational data, production data, and customer use data to name a few. But dairy farming's feedback loop makes it the perfect place to learn about how data can inform product creation and analysis.

A major hurdle data-oriented companies face when bringing Data Science into new industries is to first show them how much data they really have and how that data can inform their business decisions. Industries like agriculture produce a remarkable amount of data but hit speed bumps when it comes to collection, storage, and analysis. That's where Farmeron comes in.

"The major problem we keep on seeing — especially in bigger, modern farms — is that there's a lot of data being created and not being used, on how they're performing, what they're doing," claims Farmeron CEO Matija Kopic.

Using cloud based storage and automated setup, Farmeron provides instant access to unlimited storage. They work with farmers to utilize the data collection technology they already possess and provide software tailor-made to the industry. Their customers are loving it, and finding that data science actually provides a considerably high return on investment.

Testimonials proclaim: "Farmeron helped me boost my milk production from 54.5 lbs. to 73.1 lbs. in just under 5 months." And, "I've learned how to cut costs of my feed by 8 % with Farmeron's feed nutritional value analyzer."

Farmeron identified their niche, they found an industry untouched by Data Science that could be easily transformed by it. Analyzing the product and means of production is quite clear when it comes to cows, so let's take a look and see how product analysis works on other industries.

Why it Matters

Farmeron is just one example of a much larger trend in the Data Science industry. A lot of companies don't really need extensive Data Science abilities that come with Business Intelligence or Data Discovery tools. Instead, they just need a few simple tools tailored to their business.

The truth is that anyone in any business can benefit from using analytics, and we're all waking up to this reality. However, typical analytics tools can be rather expensive. Some installations can cost upwards of half a million dollars a year and cheap ones typically start around 50k.

If you're a dairy farmer or small business owner that type of money is impossible for you, and that is why this new market is emerging: specialized tools at a much cheaper price. If you have very specific needs or are a small business, it's worth asking people in your industry to see if there's a Farmeron for your industry that you should be looking at.

And you'd be surprised at how many industries already have tailor-made solutions ready to go. Next, for example, we'll look at some possibilities... if you run a restaurant.

Service Analytics

Have you noticed the service getting better at your favorite restaurant? How about the menu? If so, it might not be a coincidence. Restaurants across the country are dialing into the new data driven business model, and analytics is becoming as integral to daily operations as salt.

In these new data driven restaurants, every item sold, every tip received, and every moment of your restaurant experience is recorded, profiled, and analyzed. Startups like Slingshot build data solutions tailored toward the restaurant business.

The majority of restaurants are stuck in the twilight zone when it comes to data science; they rely on paper for processing and don't even take advantage of the data they do enter. The restaurant business lags behind just about every significant industry when it comes to utilizing data to increase profits and efficiency.

For a long time this was just fine, the eateries were making money and customers were happy, but as the economic downturn forced shut the doors of many businesses, restaurants finally started turning to their data. Many software systems sprang up to help track metrics like sales trends, overtime, and orders from suppliers.

Slingshot is the most comprehensive solution by far. With its unique analytics system, alongside everything else, the wait staff is getting a big data boost.

"It used to be that a manager would say, 'That server's great! He's a nice guy, he shows up on time and keeps the salt shakers full,'" says Damian

Mogavero, the man behind Slingshot. "Now they can tell a server, 'You sell 40 percent less red wine than your peers and you work in a steakhouse!'"

This change is powered by transaction data. Your order is entered instantly into the computer system and is analyzed for trends and anomalies. This change to data driven business is another example of how companies are building Analytics tools tailored to small business needs.

Part 4: The Future of Data Science and Big Data

Section 4.1: The Future of Big Data

We are in the midst of a seismic shift in the Data Science world. Industries are waking up to the reality that data is an asset, and not a simple storage necessity. This is a shift from "here, this needs to be done—go take care of it for me" to "how do I unlock the value in this?". Not everyone has yet woken up to this new business opportunity, but as they do, they'll gain distinct advantages within their industries.

This realization is beginning to manifest itself in the marketplace, with the newer analytics tools focusing more on deriving insight from data than running reports and dashboards. Which is of course, the correct way to look at this problem or any problem—focus on the end goal, don't focus on the "how": keep your eye on the prize.

However, the tools available today are primarily old-school business intelligence tools that are being retrofitted as fast as possible to try to ride this wave. Whether or not they will actually succeed or a new generation of tools will need to emerge is still an open question.

With that in mind here are 5 developmental directions to watch:

Your Data will tell you what is Interesting

Current Business Intelligence does exactly the opposite: you tell your tool what you're interested in. The coming generation will tell you what's interesting. Way back in the beginning of this book we discussed the importance of this, the importance of generating "Data Intelligence".

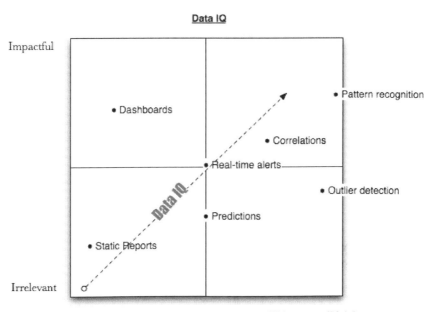

Data IQ

Impactful

- Dashboards
- Pattern recognition
- Correlations
- Real-time alerts
- Outlier detection
- Predictions
- Static Reports

Irrelevant

Things you already knew   Things you didn't know

Generating these types of insights will become much easier in the coming years and personalization will have a lot to do with this. Think about how revolutionary Pandora was for music when you first tried it—it actually learns what you find interesting! This is the direction analytics is heading.

The systems themselves will also get better at automatic learning and pattern recognition—about what you want to see. This will enable them to spot outliers, trend changes, and other interesting data that, today, must be spotted by a human being.

Wild Visualizations

Charts and graphs have been around for a long time. And there's a reason for that: they're good at conveying meaning in an easy-to-grasp way.

But again, they were developed as a way to understand much smaller amounts of data than we're looking at now. New ways of looking at data—and especially interacting with it—are being developed. Right now we're seeing the first wave of this, where designers are trying things out and some work, some don't. Things like infographics, interactive Web pages, and some of the newer intelligence tools are examples of trying new ways of looking at data.

We expect to see this trend accelerate. And as the field becomes more popular and more vital to the world economy, the brains and time spent on this problem will lead to breakthroughs in new ways to look at and understand data.

Self-Serve Intelligence

The ability to use analytics will no longer be a specialized skill, and we are already seeing the beginnings of this with Data Discovery tools. It will be a common and everyday thing for executives on down the line to use as part of their daily and hourly workflow. We've seen how this is playing out through IBM's Watson and it will be especially pervasive in the knowledge industry.

This is slightly counter-intuitive because the amount of data being used is growing by the day, and yet the tools will be simpler? Yes, that's right.

As the amount of data increases it is forcing a complete reevaluation of what intelligence tools need to be. The complex user interfaces with miles of toolbars and byzantine menu systems are no longer adequate—they were built for a world with much less data.

Which brings us to the new types of interfaces that are needed:

Natural and Intuitive Data Interaction

Business intelligence is one of the last bastions of enterprise-y software simply because of its complexity. You know you're using business intelligence software if half the screen is taken by menus and a passerby would have no idea what you're looking at.

Natural interfaces such as touch, voice, and gestures abstract away the complexity. The more functionality you can make intuitive the more productive a user can be, because they won't have to learn how to use it. When you can literally ask the question "what demographic should I focus on to increase sales?" You can find valuable information without training or expert help.

Apple did the world a great service by training people to use touch and coming up with intuitive—and, now, universally accepted—touch gestures. Apple's Siri is important because it is training people to use voice. Microsoft's Kinect is important because it's training people to use body gestures. All of these modes of input combined create an interactive environment that lets you play with your data—explore it and interact with it.

You will think with your eyes and follow your nose to the data you're looking for, even if you're not sure of the right question to ask.

Data will be **fun**.

Collaborative

A few years ago you couldn't escape "collaboration" as a buzzword. The idea was that by enabling people to work together you freed them to pool their creative and mental resources. Hopefully, of course, resulting in a synergistic explosion of ideas and good decisions.

Collaboration was, in a sense, a way to deal with a lot of information—Big Data—before Big Data got really Big. Crowd-sourced report hunting, basically. Unfortunately the amount of data that needs to be evaluated is simply too big even for large numbers of people to efficiently look at.

The new types of interfaces (as explained above) will alleviate that problem. But there was a core value in collaboration that doesn't go away just because it's no longer "the new black". Two heads are still better than one, if they're in the right place at the right time.

When tools allow people to use intuitive interfaces to not only explore their data and discover from it but also to allow more than one person to do this at the same time, the results will be nothing short of magical. Imagine being able to look at data in interesting ways, exploring it and sharing what you're looking at in real-time with colleagues from around the world. Igniting conversations. Enabling people to work on the same thing but giving them the freedom to explore independently gives you the best of both worlds.

When is the future?

Most of these changes will happen within the next 3 to 5 years. Some of them are happening already. But all signs point to a type of inevitability for them— they are at the intersection of two or more larger trends driving our society towards a new type of information consumption. One that's very different from what you think of today.

Thank you

That's the end of the book. We'd like to thank you for hanging in there with us, and we hope you've learned a thing or two. Best of luck in all your data endeavors, we'd love nothing more than to include you as a case study in an updated version of this book!

You found the secret page

Applied Data Labs has a secret. We've been working on a brand new product for the past two years that makes getting value out of your data easier than it's ever been. Basically all of the heavy lifting we talked about in this book—it does it behind the scenes. We are really excited about it.

The product is called Touchdata, and we think it's truly revolutionary. As you import data (which it takes care of storing) it measures it in a variety of ways so that it can run advanced statistical analysis on the fly. Not only that, but it then presents those insights to you in a beautiful dynamic tablet app, and allows you to drill into and explore your data using simply touch and voice.

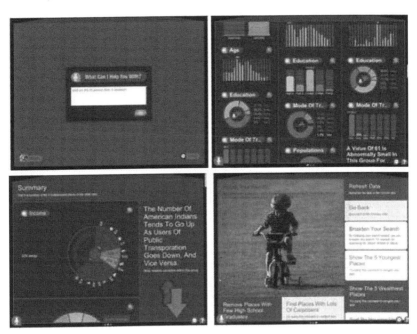

Sexy, no?

128

This technology isn't available publicly yet—you won't find it by looking around our Web site. But if this sounds interesting to you let us know and we'll put you on our VIP First Wave List where you'll be among the first to have the opportunity to sign up.

gettouchdata.com

Appendix A: Additional Resources

Part 1
1.4

In-depth introduction to Markov Chain Analysis
http://qmrg.org.uk/files/2008/11/1-intro-markov-chain-analysis2.pdf

1.5

Advanced data science email list: subscribe to our mailing list.

1.6

The Nitty Gritty of building a recomender algorithm: Amazon.com Recommendations: Item-to-Item Collaborative Filtering

1.7

Report on Rio Salado Community College Student Retention Program

Part 2
2.1

More from Dr. Weigend go to www.weigend.com and subscribe to his youtube channel Social Data Revolution.

2.3

Data Marts

Infochimps is perhaps the leading data marketplace, offering data on everything from Twitter to energy consumption.
Microsoft Azure Data Market offers many different types of data including real estate, transportation, consumer goods, and many more.

Pew Research, the famous survey-taking company that is often quoted on the news, offers many of its data sets for download and use.

2.4

http://hadoop.apache.org/

http://storm-project.net/

2.7

Natural Language toolkits:

> Apache OpenNLP
>
> NLTK
>
> Stanford
>
> LingPipe

Part 3

Data Discovery 2012 Roundup

Gartner Business Intelligence Report 2013

Be sure to visit our resource page at:

http://www.applieddatalabs.com/content/additional-resources

Appendix B: Term Glossary

Ad Hoc Query
A data query issued in response to an immediate need requiring instant feedback.

Affinity Analysis
See Recommender Algorithm

Aggregate data
Data combined from multiple sources.

Basket Analysis
See Recommender Algorithm

Big Data
Umbrella buzzword under which a wide range of advancements in data management reside.

Cloud Computing
One form of computing as a service, often providing analytics services without requiring onsite installation.

Conversion Identifier
A value within a dataset that allows it to be joined with another related dataset.

Correlation
A value ranging from 1 to -1 that indicates the level to which two variables or values move together.

CRM (Customer Relationship Management)
CRM software provides basic BI abilities to small businesses

Dashboards
An old means of keeping track of data that presented groups of important data selected by the user.

Data
Anything that can be translated into a language a computer can understand.

Data Analysis
Using statistics, with or without the aid of computerized tools, to analyze data.

Data Analytics
Using statistics and data science tools to analyze data.

Data Cleaning
The removal of mistakes from a dataset.

Data Clusters
Groupings of data around particular characteristics.

Data Consumerization
The process of making data easy to use.

Data Cruncher
Any tool that helps people do data analytics.

Data Discovery
The analytics driven ability to play with data and find unique and valuable information.

Data Drilling
Breaking data into its component parts in order to gain greater insight. (days to hours, hours to minutes, etc.)

Data Intelligence
Clear usable information gathered through data analysis.

Data Mining
Designing of new processes for creating useful data intelligence.

Data Normalization
The act of changing the structure of different data sets so that they match. (Illinois –to- IL)

Data Pipeline
The process data goes through in order to be analyzed.

Data Query
The information (a question) sent to analytics software in order to gather data knowledge (an answer).

Data Reporting
The task of turning a data query into data knowledge that is now performed by analytics.

Data Semi – Structured
Data that has a structure under unstructured information.

Data Set
A collection of facts and figures, commonly in spreadsheet form, submitted to a program for analysis.

Data Story
The idea that, when understood properly, data tells useful stories.

Data Structured
Data that is fully suitable to be used by Analytics tools.

Data Unstructured
Information like video or text that requires translation prior to analysis.

Data Visualization
An emerging trend in analytics that enables easier proportional and relational analysis through the use of charts, graphs, and infographics.

Data Warehousing
The storing and managing of large amounts of data.

Data Wrangling
The skill of making various datasets work together well.

Database
A data storage center.

Decision Automation

New technology that enables analytics systems to make changes to optimize performance.

ERP (Enterprise Resource Planning)
Company wide uniform data management system providing real time data tracing and often automated decision making tools.

ETL (Extract Transform Load)
The process of taking data from an outside source, converting it to fit current standardization, and adding it to current data.

HOLAP (Hybrid Online Analytical Processing)
Combination of ROLAP (relational) and MOLAP (multidimensional) enabling higher degrees of control and data manipulation for the user.

Infographic
A data presentation style that aims to make data appealing to look at and visually punchy.

Insights
The truths hidden in data that can be used to improve the way a business in run.

Interactive Reporting
Data reporting tools with high levels of data discovery easily accessible.

KPI (Key Performance Indicators)
User selected data streams that indicate overall success. Typically a key component of dashboards.

KSI (Key Success Indicators)
See KPI

Machine Learning algorithms
Algorithms that can learn from a given set of data, what to look for in other data.

MOLAP (Multidimensional Online Analytical Processing)
The more traditional form means of data storage for OLAP, faster processing but less data storage ability.

MetaData
The concept of data about data, most easily understood as reference tools.

Multidimensional Analysis
Data visualization demonstrating multiple factors of importance (volume and time, profit margin, expenses, revenue, time, etc.)

Multivariate Testing
Hypothesis testing on complex multi-variable systems.

Natural Language Processing (NLP)
The tools used to add structure to written or spoken language.

OLAP Online Analytical Processing
A technical term referring to specific background structures of analytics within cloud computing.

Outlier Detection
The identification of statistically valid deviations from the established norm for a given entity.

Pattern recognition
The process of Identifying and analyzing patterns within data.

Predictions
The process of making estimations of probable outcomes based on current data.

Real Time Alerts
Scorecard tool that enables you to receive instant notification if preset data values happen.

Recommender Algorithm
An Algorithm that analyzes patterns in data to find correlations that provide recommendations. Example: Amazon's "also bought" or "also viewed".

RDBMS (Relational Database Management System)
The technology enabling more rational organization of data.

ROLAP (Relational Online Analytical Processing)
A means of data storage that enables far greater amounts of data storage.

Root Cause Analysis
The process by which analytics identifies the initial cause of a statistical anomaly.

Scorecard
A data report tracking KPI's and comparing current level with set goals. Does not provide information on how to attain the goals however.

Sequence Clustering Algorithm
an algorithm that attempts to find common paths, or sequences, which lead to specific events.

Static Reports
Reports about data that are ordered, then processed and delivered.

Statistically Valid
A measure used to determine if a particular result is worth acting upon.

Statistics
The principles of data manipulation that are the driving force in data science.

Theoretical Analytics
The branch of analytical science focused on the expansion of analytical computing abilities.

Training Data
A set of data that has been classified as good, and is then used to train an algorithm to classifiy similar types of data.

Made in the USA
San Bernardino, CA
28 April 2017